Willkommen!

Just Enough **German**

D. L. Ellis, A. Cheyne

Pronunciation **Dr. J. Baldwin**

PASSPORT BOOKS

Trade Imprint of National Textbook Company
Lincolnwood, Illinois U.S.A.

The publishers would like to thank the
Austrian, German and Swiss National Tourist Offices for their help
during the preparation of this book

1987 Printing

This edition first published in 1983 by Passport Books, Trade
Imprint of National Textbook Company, 4255 West Touhy
Avenue, Lincolnwood, Illinois 60646-1975 U.S.A.

67890RD 9876

Contents

Using the phrase book

- Though primarily designed to help you get by in Germany, to get what you want or need, this phrase book would also be of use to travelers to Austria and Switzerland. It concentrates on the simplest but most effective way you can express these needs in an unfamiliar language.
- The CONTENTS on p. 5 give you a good idea of which section to consult for the phrase you need.
- The INDEX on p. 155 gives more detailed information about where to look for your phrase.
- When you have found the right page you will be given:
  either — the exact phrase
  or — help in making up a suitable sentence
  and — help to get the pronunciation right
- The English sentences in **bold type** will be useful for you in a variety of different situations, so they are worth learning by heart. (See also DO IT YOURSELF, p. 145.)
- Wherever possible you will find help in understanding what German-speaking people say to *you*, in reply to your questions.
- If you want to practise the basic nuts and bolts of the language further, look at the DO IT YOURSELF section starting on p. 145.
- Note especially these three sections:
  Everyday expressions p. 11
  Shop talk p. 57
  Public notices p. 123
  You are sure to want to refer to them most frequently.
- Once abroad, remember to make good use of the local tourist offices (see p. 24).

US addresses:

German National Tourist Office
747 Third Avenue
33rd Floor
New York, NY 10017
(212) 308-3300

Swiss National Tourist Office
608 Fifth Avenue
New York, NY 10020
(212) 757-5944

Austrian National Tourist Office
545 Fifth Avenue
New York, NY 10017
(800) 223-0284

A note on the pronunciation system

In traveler's phrase books there is usually a pronunciation section which tries to teach English-speaking tourists how to correctly pronounce the language of the country they are visiting. This is based on the belief that in order to be understood, the speaker must have an accurate, authentic accent—that he must pronounce every last word letter-perfectly.

The authors of this book, on the other hand, wanted to devise a workable and usable pronunciation system. So they had to face the fact it is absolutely impossible for an average speaker of English who has no technical training in phonetics and phonetic transcription systems (which includes 98% of all the users of this book!) to reproduce the sounds of a foreign language with perfect accuracy, just from reading a phonetic transcription, cold—no prior background in the language. We also believe that you don't have to have perfect pronunciation in order to make yourself understood in a foreign country. After all, natives you run into will take into account that you are foreigners, and visitors, and more than likely they will feel gratified by your efforts to communicate and will probably go out of their way to try to understand you. They may even help you, and correct you, in a friendly manner. We have found, also, that visitors to a foreign country are not usually concerned with perfect pronunciation—they just want to get their message across, to communicate!

With this in mind, we have designed a pronunciation system which is of the utmost simplicity to use. This system does not attempt to give an accurate—but also problematical and tedious—representation of the sound system of the language, but instead uses common sound and letter combinations in English which are the closest to the sounds in the foreign language. In this way, the sentences transcribed for pronunciation should be read as naturally as possible, as if they were ordinary English. In no way does the user have to attempt to make the words sound "foreign." So, while to yourselves you will sound as if you are speaking ordinary English—or at least making ordinary English sounds—you will at the same time be making yourselves understood in another language. And, as the saying goes, practice makes perfect, so it is probably a good idea to repeat aloud to yourselves several times the phrases you think you are going to use, before you actually use them. This will give you greater confidence, and will also help in making yourself understood.

In German it is important to stress or emphasize the syllables in italics, just as you would if we were to take as an English example: *li*ttle Jack Horner s*a*t in the *co*rner. Here we have ten syllables, but only four stresses.

Of course you may enjoy trying to pronounce a foreign language as well as possible and the present system is a good way to start. However, since it uses only the sounds of English, you will very soon need to depart from it as you imitate the sounds you hear the native speaker produce and begin to relate them to the spelling of the other language. German will pose no problems as there is an obvious and consistent relationship between pronunciation and spelling.

Viel Spass!

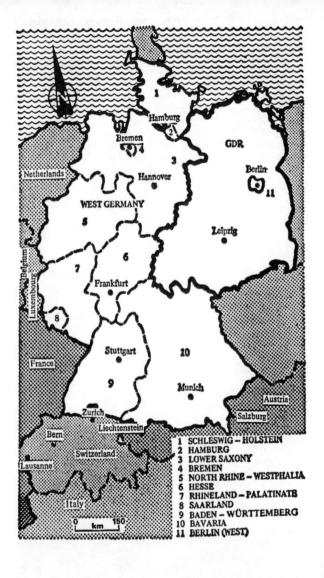

1 SCHLESWIG – HOLSTEIN
2 HAMBURG
3 LOWER SAXONY
4 BREMEN
5 NORTH RHINE – WESTPHALIA
6 HESSE
7 RHINELAND – PALATINATE
8 SAARLAND
9 BADEN – WÜRTTEMBERG
10 BAVARIA
11 BERLIN (WEST)

Everyday expressions

[See also 'Shop talk', p. 57]

Hello	**Guten Tag**
	goo-ten tahk
Hello (Austria)	**Grüss Gott**
	grooss got
Good morning	**Guten Morgen**
	goo-ten morgen
Good day	**Guten Tag**
Good afternoon	goo-ten tahk
Good evening	**Guten Abend**
	goo-ten ah-bent
Good night	**Gute Nacht**
	goo-teh nakt
Good-bye	**Auf Wiedersehn**
	owf veeder-zain
	Tschüss (friends only)
	choos
See you later	**Bis später**
	bis shpater
Yes	**Ja**
	yah
Please	**Bitte**
	bitteh
Yes, please	**Ja, bitte**
	yah bitteh
Great!	**Prima!**
	pree-mah
Thank you	**Danke**
	dankeh
Thank you very much	**Vielen Dank**
	feelen dank
That's right	**Das stimmt**
	das shtimmt
No	**Nein**
	nine
No, thank you	**Nein, danke**
	nine dankeh
I disagree	**Das stimmt nicht**
	das shtimmt nisht

Excuse me Sorry	**Entschuldigen Sie** ent-sh*oo*l-dig-en zee
Don't mention it That's OK	**Bitte sehr** b*i*tteh zair
That's good I like it	**Das gefällt mir** das ga-f*e*llt meer
That's no good I don't like it	**Das gefällt mir nicht** das ga-f*e*llt meer n*i*sht
I know	**Ich weiss** ish v*i*ce
I don't know	**Ich weiss nicht** ish v*i*ce nisht
It doesn't matter	**Es macht nichts** es m*a*kt n*i*shts
Where's the toilet, please?	**Wo sind die Toiletten?** v*o* zint dee twa-l*e*tten
How much is that? [*point*]	**Wieviel kostet das?** vee-feel k*o*stet das
Is the service included?	**Ist die Bedienung inbegriffen?** ist dee bed*ee*-noong *i*n-beg-riffen
Do you speak English?	**Sprechen Sie Englisch?** shpreshen zee *e*ng-lish
I'm sorry ...	**Es tut mir leid ...** es t*oo*t meer l*i*te ...
I don't speak German	**ich spreche nicht Deutsch** ish shpr*e*sheh nisht d*o*ytsh
I only speak a little German	**ich spreche nur ein wenig Deutsch** ish shpr*e*sheh noor ine v*a*y-nik d*o*ytsh
I don't understand	**ich verstehe nicht** ish fer-sht*a*y-heh nisht
Please can you ...	**Bitte können Sie ...** b*i*tteh k*e*rnnen zee ...
repeat that?	**das wiederholen?** das v*ee*der-h*o*len
speak more slowly?	**langsamer sprechen?** l*a*ng-zahmer shpr*e*shen
write it down?	**das aufschreiben?** das *o*wf-shr*y*-ben
What is this called in German? [*point*]	**Wie heisst das auf Deutsch?** vee h*y*sst das owf d*o*ytsh

Crossing the border

ESSENTIAL INFORMATION

- Don't waste time just before you leave rehearsing what you're going to say to the border officials – the chances are that you won't have to say anything at all, especially if you travel by air.
- It's more useful to check that you have your documents handy for the journey: passport, tickets, money, travellers' cheques, insurance documents, driving licence and car registration documents.
- Look out for these signs:
  ZOLL (customs)
  GRENZE (border)
  GRENZPOLIZEI (frontier police)
  [*For further signs and notices, see p. 123*]
- You may be asked routine questions by the customs officials [*see below*]. If you have to give personal details see 'Meeting people', p. 15. The other important answer to know is 'Nothing': **Nichts** (nishts).

ROUTINE QUESTIONS

Passport?	**Pass?** pass
Insurance?	**Versicherungskarte?** fer-zisher-oongs-karteh
Registration document? (logbook)	**Kraftfahrzeugschein?** kraft-far-tsoyk-shine
Ticket, please	**Fahrkarte, bitte** far-karteh bitteh
Have you anything to declare?	**Haben Sie etwas zu verzollen?** hahben zee etvas tsoo fer-tsollen
Where are you going?	**Wohin fahren Sie?** vo-hin far-en zee
How long are you staying?	**Wie lange bleiben Sie?** vee lang-eh bly-ben zee
Where have you come from?	**Woher kommen Sie?** vo-hair kommen zee

14/Crossing the border

You may also have to fill in forms which ask for:

surname	**(Familien–) Name**
first name	**Vorname**
maiden name	**Mädchenname**
place of birth	**Geburtsort**
date of birth	**Geburtsdatum**
address	**Adresse/Anschrift**
nationality	**Staatsangehörigkeit**
profession	**Beruf**
passport number	**Passnummer**
issued at	**ausgestellt in**
signature	**Unterschrift**

Meeting people

[See also 'Everyday expressions', p. 11]

Breaking the ice

Hello	**Guten Tag (Hallo)**
	goo-ten tahk (hullo)
Hello (Austria)	**Grüss Gott**
	grooss got
Good morning	**Guten Morgen**
	goo-ten morgen
How are you?	**Wie geht es Ihnen? (Wie geht's?)**
	vee gait es *ee*nen (vee gaits)

[Expressions above in brackets should only be used with people you know well.]

Pleased to meet you	**Angenehm**
	un-ga-name
I am here ...	**Ich bin hier ...**
	ish bin here ...
on holiday	**auf Urlaub**
	owf *oor*-lowp
on business	**auf Geschäftsreise**
	owf gas*hefts*-ryzeh
Can I offer you ...	**Kann ich Ihnen ... anbieten?**
	kan ish *ee*nen ... *an*-beeten
a drink?	**etwas zu trinken**
	*et*vas tsoo tr*i*nken
a cigarette?	**eine Zigarette**
	*i*neh tsee-gar*e*tteh
a cigar?	**eine Zigarre**
	*i*neh tsee-g*a*rreh
Are you staying long?	**Bleiben Sie hier lange?**
	bl*y*-ben zee here lang-eh

Name

What's your name?	**Wie ist Ihr Name?**
	vee ist eer n*a*hmeh
My name is ...	**Mein Name ist ...**
	mine n*a*hmeh ist ...

Family

Are you married?	**Sind Sie verheiratet?** zint zee fer-hy-rah-tet
I am ...	**Ich bin ...** ish bin ...
married	**verheiratet** fer-hy-rah-tet
single	**ledig** *laid*-ik
This is ...	**Dies ist ...** *dees* ist ...
my wife	**meine Frau** *mineh* fr*ow*
my husband	**mein Mann** mine m*unn*
my son	**mein Sohn** mine *zone*
my daughter	**meine Tochter** *mineh* t*okter*
my (boy) friend	**mein Freund** mine fr*oynt*
my (girl) friend	**meine Freundin** *mineh* fr*oyndin*
my (male) colleague	**mein Kollege** mine col-l*aig*-eh
my (female) colleague	**meine Kollegin** *mineh* col-l*aig*-in
Do you have any children?	**Haben Sie Kinder?** h*ah*ben zee k*in*-der
I have ...	**Ich habe ...** ish h*ah*beh ...
one daughter	**eine Tochter** *in*eh t*oshter*
one son	**einen Sohn** *in*en *zone*
two daughters	**zwei Töchter** tsvy t*ershter*
three sons	**drei Söhne** dry *zerneh*
No, I haven't any children	**Nein, ich habe keine Kinder** nine ish h*ah*beh k*in*eh k*in*-der

Where you live

Are you ...	Sind Sie ... zint zee ...
German?	**Deutscher/Deutsche?*** doyt-sher/doyt-sheh
Austrian?	**Österreicher/Österreicherin?*** erster-ryker/erster-ryker-in
Swiss?	**Schweizer/Schweizerin?*** shvytser/shvytser-in
I am ...	**Ich bin ...** ish bin ...
American	**Amerikaner/Amerikanerin*** ameri-kah-ner/ameri-kah-ner-in
English	**Engländer/Engländerin*** eng-lender/eng-lender-in

[*For other nationalities, see p. 138*]

* For men use the first word, for women the second.

Where are you from?

I'm ...	Ich bin ... ish bin ...
from London	**aus London** ows london
from England	**aus England** ows eng-lant
from the north	**aus dem Norden** ows dem norden
from the south	**aus dem Süden** ows dem zooden
from the east	**aus dem Osten** ows dem osten
from the west	**aus dem Westen** ows dem vesten
from the centre	**aus dem Zentrum (des Landes)** ows dem tsent-room (des land-es)

[*For other countries, see p. 137*]

For the businessman and woman

I'm from ... (firm's name)	**Ich bin von ...** ish bin fon ...
I have an appointment with ...	**Ich habe eine Verabredung mit ...** ish hahbeh ineh fer-up-ray-doong mit ...
May I speak to ... ?	**Kann ich ... sprechen?** kan ish ... shpreshen
This is my card	**Hier ist meine Karte** here ist mineh karteh
I'm sorry, I'm late	**Es tut mir leid, ich habe mich verspätet** es toot meer lite ish hahbeh mish fer-shpay-tet
Can I fix another appointment?	**Kann ich eine neue Verabredung treffen?** kan ish ineh noy-eh fer-up-ray-doong treffen
I'm staying at the (Crown) hotel	**Ich wohne im Hotel (Krone)** ish vone-eh im hotel (krone-eh)
I'm staying in (Park) Road	**Ich wohne in der (Park) strasse** ish vone-eh in der (park) shtrahsseh

Asking the way

ESSENTIAL INFORMATION

● Keep a look out for all these place names as you will find them on shops, maps and notices.

WHAT TO SAY

Excuse me, please	**Entschuldigen Sie, bitte**
	ent-shool-dig-en zee bitteh
How do I get . . .	**Wie komme ich . . .**
	vee kommeh ish . . .
to Hamburg?	**nach Hamburg?**
	nahk hum-boork
to (Station) Road?	**zur (Bahnhof)strasse?**
	tsoor (bahn-hof-)shtrahsseh
to the hotel (Krone)?	**zum Hotel (Krone)?**
	tsoom hotel (krone-eh)
to the airport?	**zum Flughafen?**
	tsoom flook-hahfen
to the beach?	**zum Strand?**
	tsoom shtrant
to the bus station?	**zum Busbahnhof?**
	tsoom boos-bahn-hof
to the historic site?	**zur historischen Stätte?**
	tsoor histo-rish-en shtetteh
to the market?	**zum Markt?**
	tsoom markt
to the police station?	**zur Polizeiwache**
	tsoor poli-tsy-vakkeh
to the port?	**zum Hafen?**
	tsoom hahfen
to the post office?	**zum Postamt?**
	tsoom post-amt
to the railway station?	**zum Bahnhof?**
	tsoom bahn-hof
to the sports stadium?	**zum Stadion?**
	tsoom shtah-dee-on

How do I get ...

Wie komme ich ...
vee kommeh ish ...

to the tourist information office?
zum Fremdenverkehrsbüro?
tsoom fremden-ferkairs-buro

to the town centre?
zum Stadtzentrum?
tsoom shtatt-tsent-room

to the town hall?
zum Rathaus?
tsoom raht-house

Excuse me, please
Entschuldigen Sie, bitte
ent-shool-dig-en zee bitteh

Is there ... near by?
Gibt es ... in der Nähe?
geept es ... in der nay-eh

an art gallery
eine Kunstgalerie
ineh koonst-galeree

a baker's
eine Bäckerei
ineh becker-ry

a bank
eine Bank
ineh bank

a bar
eine Bar
ineh bar

a botanical garden
einen botanischen Garten
inen botah-nishen garten

a bus stop
eine Bushaltestelle
ineh boos-halteh-shtelleh

a butcher's
eine Metzgerei
ineh mets-ga-ry

a café
ein Café
ine caffay

a cake shop
eine Konditorei
ineh con-dee-to-ry

a campsite
einen Campingplatz
inen camping-plats

a car park
einen Parkplatz
inen park-plats

a change bureau
eine Wechselstube
ineh veksel-shtoobeh

a chemist's
eine Apotheke
ineh ah-potake-eh

a church
eine Kirche
ineh keer-sheh

a cinema
ein Kino
ine kee-no

a delicatessen	**ein Feinkostgeschäft**
	*i*ne *f*ine-kost-gash*e*ft
a dentist's	**einen Zahnarzt**
	*i*nen ts*a*hn-artst
a department store	**ein Kaufhaus**
	*i*ne k*o*wf-house
a disco	**eine Diskothek**
	*i*neh disco-t*a*ke
a doctor's surgery	**eine Arztpraxis**
	*i*neh *a*rtst-prak-sis
a dry cleaner's	**eine Reinigung**
	*i*neh r*y*-nee-goong
a fishmonger's	**ein Fischgeschäft**
	*i*ne f*i*sh-gash*e*ft
a garage (for repairs)	**eine Autowerkstatt**
	*i*neh *o*wto-vairk-shtatt
a hairdresser's	**einen Frisör**
	*i*nen free-z*e*r
a greengrocer's	**eine Gemüsehandlung**
	*i*neh ga-m*oo*zeh-hant-loong
a grocer's	**ein Lebensmittelgeschäft**
	*i*ne l*a*bens-mittel-gash*e*ft
a hardware shop	**eine Eisenwarenhandlung**
	*i*neh *i*zen-vahren-handloong
a hospital	**ein Krankenhaus**
	*i*ne kr*a*nken-house
a hotel	**ein Hotel**
	*i*ne hot*e*l
an ice-cream parlour	**eine Eisdiele**
	*i*neh *i*ce-deeleh
a local sickness insurance office	**eine Krankenkasse**
	*i*neh kr*a*nken-kasseh
a laundry	**eine Wäscherei**
	*i*neh vesheh-r*y*
a museum	**ein Museum**
	*i*ne moo-z*a*y-oom
a newsagent's	**einen Zeitungshändler**
	*i*nen ts*y*-toongs-hentler
a night club	**einen Nachtklub**
	*i*nen n*a*kt-kloop
a park	**einen Park**
	*i*nen p*a*rk

Is there . . . near by?   **Gibt es . . . in der Nähe?**
geept es . . . in der nay-eh

a petrol station   **eine Tankstelle**
ineh tank-shtelleh

a post box   **einen Briefkasten**
inen breef-kasten

a public telephone   **eine Telefonzelle**
ineh telefone-tselleh

a public toilet   **öffentliche Toiletten**
erffent-lish-eh twa-letten

a restaurant   **ein Restaurant**
ine rest-o-rung

a snack bar   **einen Schnellimbiss**
inen shnell-im-bis

a sports ground   **einen Sportplatz**
inen shport-plats

a supermarket   **einen Supermarkt**
inen zooper-markt

a sweet shop   **einen Süsswarenladen**
inen zooss-vahren-lahden

a swimming pool   **ein Schwimmbad**
ine shvimm-baht

a taxi stand   **einen Taxistand**
inen taxi-shtant

a theatre   **ein Theater**
ine tay-ahter

a tobacconist's   **einen Zigarettenladen**
inen tsee-garetten-lahden

a travel agent's   **ein Reisebüro**
ine ryzeh-buro

a youth hostel   **eine Jugendherberge**
ineh yoogent-hair-bairgeh

a zoo   **einen Zoo**
inen tso

DIRECTIONS

- Asking where a place is, or if a place is near by, is one thing; making sense of the answer is another.
- Here are some of the most important key directions and replies.

Left	**Links**
	links
Right	**Rechts**
	reshts
Straight on	**Geradeaus**
	grahdeh-ows
There	**Dort**
	dort
First left/right	**Erste Strasse links/rechts**
	airsteh shtrahsseh links/reshts
Second left/right	**Zweite Strasse links/ rechts**
	tsvy-teh shtrahsseh links/reshts
At the crossroads	**Bei der Kreuzung**
	by der kroy-tsoong
At the traffic lights	**Bei der Ampel**
	by der umpel
At the roundabout	**Beim Kreisverkehr**
	bime krice-fer-kair
At the level-crossing	**Beim Bahnübergang**
	bime bahn-oober-gang
It's near/far	**Es ist nah/weit**
	es ist nah/vite
One kilometre	**Ein Kilometer**
	ine kilo-mater
Two kilometres	**Zwei Kilometer**
	tsvy kilo-mater
Five minutes ...	**Fünf Minuten ...**
	foonf minooten ...
on foot	**zu Fuss**
	tsoo fooss
by car	**mit dem Auto**
	mit dem owto
Take ...	**Nehmen Sie ...**
	nay-men zee ...
the bus	**den Bus**
	den booss
the train	**den Zug**
	den tsook
the tram	**die Strassenbahn**
	dee shtrahssen-bahn
the underground	**die U–Bahn**
[*For public transport, see p. 114*]	dee oo-bahn

The tourist information office

ESSENTIAL INFORMATION

- Most towns and holiday resorts in Germany, Switzerland and Austria have a tourist information office; in smaller towns the local travel agent (REISEBÜRO) provides the same information and services.
- Look for these words:
  FREMDENVERKEHRSBÜRO
  VERKEHRSAMT
  INFORMATIONSBÜRO
- If your main concern is to find and book accommodation, a **ZIMMERNACHWEIS** (room-booking office) is the best place to go to.
- Tourist offices offer you free information in the form of printed leaflets, fold-outs, brochures, lists and plans.
- You may have to pay for some types of documents but this is not usual.
- For finding a tourist office, see p. 19.

WHAT TO SAY

Please, have you got …	**Bitte, haben Sie …**
	bitteh hahben zee …
a plan of the town?	**einen Stadtplan?**
	inen shtatt-plahn
a list of events?	**einen Veranstaltungskalender**
	inen fer-un-shtaltoongs-kalender
a list of hotels?	**ein Hotelverzeichnis?**
	ine hotel-fer-tsysh-nis
a list of campsites?	**ein Campingplatzverzeichnis?**
	ine camping-plats-fer-tsysh-nis
a list of restaurants?	**ein Restaurantverzeichnis?**
	ine resto-rung-fer-tsysh-nis
a list of coach excursions?	**eine Liste mit Ausflugsfahrten?**
	ineh listeh mit ows-flooks-farten
a leaflet on the town?	**einen Prospekt von dieser Stadt?**
	inen pro-spekt fon deezer shtatt

a leaflet on the region?	**einen Prospekt von dieser Gegend?** *inen pro-spekt fon deezer gay-ghent*
a railway timetable?	**einen Zugfahrplan?** *inen tsook-far-plahn*
a bus timetable?	**einen Busfahrplan?** *inen booss-far-plahn*
In English, please	**Auf Englisch, bitte** *owf eng-lish bitteh*
How much do I owe you?	**Wieviel schulde ich Ihnen?** *vee-feel shooldeh ish eenen*
Can you recommend ...	**Können Sie ... empfehlen?** *kernnen zee ... em-pfailen*
a cheap hotel?	**ein billiges Hotel** *ine billig-es hotel*
a cheap restaurant?	**ein billiges Restaurant** *ine billig-es resto-rung*
Can you make a booking for me?	**Können Sie eine Reservierung für mich machen?** *kernnen zee ineh reser-vee-roong foor mish makhen*

LIKELY ANSWERS

You need to understand when the answer is 'No'. You should be able to tell by the assistant's facial expression, tone of voice and gesture, but there are some language clues, such as:

No	**Nein** *nine*
I'm sorry	**(Es) tut mir leid** *(es) toot meer lite*
I don't have a list of campsites	**Ich habe kein Campingplatzverzeichnis** *ish hahbeh kine camping-plats-fer-tsysh-nis*
I haven't got any left	**Ich habe keine mehr** *ish hahbeh kineh mair*
It's free	**Es ist umsonst** *es ist oom-zonst*

Accommodation

Hotel

ESSENTIAL INFORMATION

- If you want hotel-type accommodation, all the following words in capital letters are worth looking for on name boards:
  HOTEL
  HOTEL GARNI (room and breakfast, no other meals provided)
  MOTEL
  PENSION (boarding house)
  GASTHOF (inexpensive type of inn with a limited number of rooms)
  ZIMMER FREI (rooms to let in private houses, bed and breakfast)
- A list of hotels in the town or district can usually be obtained at the local tourist information office [see p. 24].
- Unlisted hotels are usually slightly cheaper and probably almost as good as listed hotels.
- Not all hotels and boarding-houses provide meals apart from breakfast; inquire about this, on arrival, at the reception.
- The cost is displayed in the room itself, so you can check it when having a look round before agreeing to stay.
- The displayed cost is for the room itself, per night and not per person. It usually includes service charges and taxes, but quite often does not include breakfast.
- Breakfast is continental style, with rolls, butter and jam; boiled eggs, cheese and cold meats are usually available on request. Some larger hotels also offer a FRÜHSTÜCKS-BUFFET where you can help yourself to cereals, yoghurt, fresh fruit etc.
- Upon arrival you will have to fill in the official registration form which bears an English translation. The receptionist will also want to see your passport.
- It is customary to tip the porter and leave a tip for the chambermaid in the hotel room.
- Finding a hotel, see p. 19.

WHAT TO SAY

I have a booking	**Ich habe reserviert**
	ish hahbeh reserveert
Have you any vacancies, please?	**Haben Sie noch Zimmer frei?**
	hahben zee nok tsimmer fry
Can I book a room?	**Kann ich ein Zimmer reservieren lassen?**
	kan ish ine tsimmer reser-veeren lassen
It's for ...	**Es ist für ...**
	es ist foor ...
one person	**eine Person**
	ineh per-zone
two people	**zwei Personen**
[For numbers, see p. 129]	tsvy per-zonen
It's for ...	**Es ist für ...**
	es ist foor ...
one night	**eine Nacht**
	ineh nakt
two nights	**zwei Nächte**
	tsvy nesh-teh
one week	**eine Woche**
	ineh vok-eh
two weeks	**zwei Wochen**
	tsvy vokken
I would like ...	**Ich möchte ...**
	ish mershteh ...
a room	**ein Zimmer**
	ine tsimmer
two rooms	**zwei Zimmer**
	tsvy tsimmer
a room with a single bed	**ein Einzelzimmer**
	ine ine-tsel-tsimmer
a room with two single beds	**ein Zweibettzimmer**
	ine tsvy-bett-tsimmer
a room with a double bed	**ein Doppelzimmer**
	ine doppel-tsimmer
I would like a room ...	**Ich möchte ein Zimmer ...**
	ish mershteh ine tsimmer ...
with a toilet	**mit Toilette**
	mit twa- letteh

I would like a room ...	**Ich möchte ein Zimmer ...**
	ish mershteh ine tsimmer ...
with a bathroom	**mit Bad**
	mit baht
with a shower	**mit Dusche**
	mit doo-sheh
with a cot	**mit einem Kinderbett**
	mit inem kin-der-bett
with a balcony	**mit Balkon**
	mit bal-kone
I would like ...	**Ich möchte ...**
	ish mershteh ...
full board	**Vollpension**
	foll-penzee-on
half board	**Halbpension**
	hal-penzee-on
bed and breakfast [see *Essential information*]	**Übernachtung mit Frühstück**
	oober-naktoong mit froo-shtok
Do you serve meals?	**Kann man bei Ihnen essen?**
	kan man by eenen essen
At what time is ...	**Wann gibt es ...**
	vann geept es ...
breakfast?	**Frühstück?**
	froo-shtook
lunch?	**Mittagessen?**
	mittahk-essen
dinner?	**Abendessen?**
	ahbent-essen
How much is it?	**Wieviel kostet es?**
	vee-feel kostet es
Can I look at the room?	**Kann ich mir das Zimmer ansehen?**
	kan ish meer das tsimmer un-zay-en
I'd prefer a room ...	**Ich hätte lieber ein Zimmer ...**
	ish hetteh leeber ine tsimmer ...
at the front/at the back	**nach vorn/nach hinten**
	nahk forn/nahk hin-ten
OK, I'll take it	**Gut, ich nehme es**
	goot ish nay-meh es
No thanks, I won't take it	**Nein, danke, ich nehme es nicht**
	nine dankeh ish nay-meh es nisht

The key to number (10), please	**Den Schlüssel für Zimmer (Zehn), bitte**
	den shl*oo*ssel foor ts*i*mmer (tsain) b*i*tteh
Please may I have ...	**Kann ich bitte ... haben?**
	k*a*n ish b*i*tteh ... h*a*hben
a coat hanger?	**einen Kleiderbügel**
	*i*nen kl*y*der-boogel
a towel?	**ein Handtuch**
	ine h*a*nt-took
a glass?	**ein Glas?**
	ine glass
some soap?	**ein Stück Seife**
	ine shtook z*y*-feh
an ashtray?	**einen Aschenbecher**
	*i*nen *a*shen-besher
another pillow?	**noch ein Kopfkissen**
	nok ine kopf-kissen
another blanket?	**noch eine Decke**
	nok *i*neh deckeh
Come in!	**Herein!**
	her-r*i*ne
One moment, please!	**Einen Moment, bitte!**
	*i*nen mo-ment b*i*tteh
Please can you ...	**Bitte, können Sie ...**
	b*i*tteh k*e*rnnen zee ...
do this laundry/dry cleaning?	**diese Sachen waschen lassen/ reinigen lassen?**
	d*ee*zeh z*a*kken v*a*shen lassen/ ry-neeg-en lassen
call me at ... ?	**mich um ... anrufen**
	mish oom ... *u*n-roofen
help me with my luggage?	**mir mit meinem Gepäck behilflich sein?**
	meer mit m*i*nem ga-peck be-h*i*lf-lish zine
call me a taxi for ... ?	**mir für ... ein Taxi bestellen?**
[*For times, see p. 131*]	meer foor ... ine t*a*xi besht*e*llen
The bill, please	**Die Rechnung, bitte**
	dee resh-noong b*i*tteh
Is service included?	**Ist Bedienung inbegriffen?**
	ist bed*ee*-noong *i*n-begriffen

I think this is wrong	**Ich glaube, hier ist ein Fehler**
	ish gla-oobeh here ist ine failer
May I have a receipt?	**Kann ich eine Quittung haben?**
	kan ish ineh kvit-oong hahben

At breakfast

Some more . . . please	**Noch etwas . . . bitte**
	nok etvas . . . bitteh
coffee	**Kaffee**
	kaffeh
tea	**Tee**
	tay
bread	**Brot**
	brote
butter	**Butter**
	bootter
jam	**Marmelade**
	marmeh-lahdeh
May I have a boiled egg?	**Kann ich ein gekochtes Ei haben?**
	kan ish ine gakokt-es eye hahben

LIKELY REACTIONS

Have you an identity document?	**Haben Sie einen Pass oder Personalausweis?**
	hahben zee inen pass oder per-zonahl-ows-vice
What's your name? [see p.15]	**Wie ist Ihr Name?**
	vee ist eer nahmeh
Sorry, we're full	**Es tut mir leid, wir sind ausgebucht**
	es toot meer lite veer zint ows-gabookt
I haven't any rooms left	**Ich habe keine Zimmer mehr frei**
	ish hahbeh kineh tsimmer mair fry
Do you want to have a look?	**Wollen Sie es sich ansehen?**
	vollen zee es zish un-zay-en
How many people is it for?	**Für wieviele Personen soll es sein?**
	foor vee-feeleh per-zonen zoll es zine

From (7 o'clock) onwards	**Ab (sieben Uhr)** up (zeeben *oo*r)
From (midday) onwards	**Ab (zwölf Uhr mittags)** up (tsverlf oor mit-tahks)
[For times, see p. 131]	
It's (40) marks	**Es kostet (vierzig) Mark** es kostet (feer-tsik) mark
[For numbers, see p. 129]	

Camping and youth hostelling

ESSENTIAL INFORMATION

Camping

- Look for the words: **CAMPINGPLATZ**
  ZELTPLATZ
- Be prepared for the following charges:
  per person
  for the car (if applicable)
  for the tent or caravan plot
  for electricity
  for hot showers
- You must provide proof of identity, such as your passport.
- If you cannot find an official camping site and want to camp elsewhere, get the permission of the farmer/landowner or the local police first.
- Camping is forbidden in the lay-bys off the motorways.
- It is usually not possible to make advance reservations on camping sites. Try and secure a site in mid-afternoon if you are travelling during the high season.
- Owners of camping sites in Germany are not liable for losses. You should make your own insurance arrangements in advance.

Youth hostels

- Look for the word **JUGENDHERBERGE**.
- You must have a YHA card.
- Your YHA card must bear your photograph; you can attach it yourself, it does not require stamping.
- There is no upper age limit at German youth hostels, except in Bavaria where the age limit is twenty-seven.
- The charge for the night is the same for all ages, but some hostels are dearer than others.
- Accommodation is usually in small dormitories.
- Many German youth hostels do *not* provide a kitchen in which visitors can prepare their own meals; but usually meals at a reasonable price are provided by the house-parents.
- You may have to help with domestic chores in some hostels.
- Finding a campsite and a youth hostel, see p. 19.
- Replacing equipment, see p. 54.

WHAT TO SAY

I have a booking	**Ich habe reserviert**
	ish hahbeh reserveert
Have you any vacancies?	**Haben Sie noch etwas frei?**
	hahben zee nok etvas fry
It's for ...	**Es ist für ...**
	es ist foor
one adult/one person	**einen Erwachsenen/eine Person**
	*i*nen er-v*a*ksen-en/*i*neh per-zone
two adults/two people	**zwei Erwachsene/zwei Personen**
	tsvy er-v*a*ksen-eh/tsvy per-z*o*nen
and one child	**und ein Kind**
	oont ine kint
and two children	**und zwei Kinder**
	oont tsvy k*i*n-der
It's for ...	**Es ist für ...**
	es ist foor ...
one night	**eine Nacht**
	*i*neh n*a*kt
two nights	**zwei Nächte**
	tsvy n*e*sh-teh

one week	eine Woche
	*i*neh v*o*k-eh
two weeks	zwei Wochen
	tsv*y* v*o*k-en
How much is it ...	Wie hoch ist die Gebühr ...
	vee hoke ist dee gab*oo*r ...
for the tent?	für das Zelt?
	foor das tselt
for the caravan?	für den Wohnwagen?
	foor den v*o*ne-vahgen
for the car?	für das Auto?
	foor das *o*wto
for the electricity?	für Elektrizität
	foor elektri-tsee-t*a*te
per person?	pro Person?
	pro per-z*o*ne
per day/night?	pro Tag/Nacht?
	pro t*a*hk/n*a*kt
May I look round?	Kann ich mich etwas umsehen?
	kan ish mish etvas *o*om-zay-en
At what time do you lock up at night?	Um wieviel Uhr schliessen Sie nachts ab?
	oom v*ee*-feel oor shl*ee*ssen zee nakts *u*p
Do you provide anything ...	Kann man bei Ihnen etwas ... bekommen?
	kan man by *ee*nen *e*tvas ... bek*o*mmen
to eat?	zu essen
	tsoo *e*ssen
to drink?	zu trinken
	tsoo tr*i*nken
Do you have ...	Haben Sie ...
	h*a*hben zee ...
a bar?	eine Bar?
	*i*neh b*a*r
hot showers?	heisse Duschen?
	hysseh d*oo*-shen
a kitchen?	eine Küche?
	*i*neh k*oo*-sheh
a launderette?	einen Waschsalon?
	*i*nen v*a*sh-zalong

Do you have ...	**Haben Sie ...**
	hahben zee ...
a restaurant?	**ein Restaurant?**
	ine resto-rung
a shop?	**ein Geschäft?**
	ine gasheft
a swimming pool?	**ein Schwimmbad?**
	ine shvimm-baht
a snack-bar?	**eine Imbisstube?**
	ineh im-bis-shtoobeh

[*For food shopping, see p. 61, and for eating and drinking out, see p. 80*]

Where are ...	**Wo sind ...**
	vo zint ...
the dustbins?	**die Abfalleimer?**
	dee up-fall-imer
the showers?	**die Duschen?**
	dee doo-shen
the toilets?	**die Toiletten?**
	dee twa-letten
At what time must one ...	**Um wieviel Uhr muss man ...**
	oom vee-feel oor mooss man ...
go to bed?	**schlafen gehen?**
	shlah-fen gain
get up?	**aufstehen?**
	owf-shtain
Please have you got ...	**Bitte haben Sie vielleicht ...**
	bitteh hahben zee fee-lysht ...
a broom?	**einen Besen?**
	inen bay-zen
a corkscrew?	**einen Korkenzieher?**
	inen korken-tsee-er
a drying-up cloth?	**ein Geschirrtuch?**
	ine gasheer-took
a fork?	**eine Gabel?**
	ineh gah-bel
a fridge?	**einen Kühlschrank?**
	inen kool-shrank

a frying pan?	**eine Bratpfanne?**
	*i*neh br*a*ht-fun-eh
an iron?	**ein Bügeleisen?**
	*i*ne b*oo*gel-*i*zen
a knife?	**ein Messer?**
	*i*ne *me*sser
a plate?	**einen Teller?**
	*i*nen *te*ller
a saucepan?	**einen Kochtopf?**
	*i*nen k*o*k-topf
a teaspoon?	**einen Teelöffel?**
	*i*nen t*a*y-lerffel
a tin opener?	**einen Dosenöffner?**
	*i*nen d*o*ze-en-erffner
any washing powder?	**Waschpulver?**
	*v*ash-poolver
any washing-up liquid?	**ein Spülmittel?**
	*i*ne shp*oo*l-mittel
The bill, please	**Die Rechnung, bitte**
	dee r*e*sh-noong b*i*tteh

Problems

The toilet	**Die Toilette**
	dee twa-l*e*tteh
The shower	**Die Dusche**
	dee d*oo*-sheh
The tap	**Der Wasserhahn**
	der v*a*sser-hahn
The razor point	**Die Steckdose für den Rasierapparat**
	dee sht*e*ck-doze-eh foor den raz*ee*r-appar*a*ht
The light	**Das Licht**
	das l*i*sht
... is not working	**... funktioniert nicht**
	... foonk-tsee-o-n*ee*rt nisht
My camping gas has run out	**Ich habe kein Camping-Gas mehr**
	ish h*a*hbeh kine c*a*mping-gahs m*ai*r

LIKELY REACTIONS

Have you an identity document?	**Haben Sie einen Pass oder Personalausweis?** h*a*hben zee *i*nen p*a*ss od*e*r per-zon*a*hl-ows-vice
Your membership card, please	**Ihre Mitgliedskarte, bitte** *ee*reh m*i*t-gleets-karteh b*i*tteh
What's your name [see p.15]	**Wie ist Ihr Name?** vee ist eer n*a*hmeh
Sorry, we're full	**Es tut mir leid, wir sind voll besetzt** es toot meer l*i*te veer zint f*o*ll bezetst
How many people is it for?	**Für wieviele Personen?** foor v*ee*-feeleh per-zonen
How many nights is it for?	**Für wieviele Nächte?** foor v*ee*-feeleh n*e*sh-teh
It's (4) marks ...	**Es kostet (vier) Mark ...** es k*o*stet (f*ee*r) m*a*rk ...
per day/per night	**pro Tag/pro Nacht** pro t*a*hk/pro n*a*kt

[For numbers, see p. 129]

Rented accommodation: problem solving

ESSENTIAL INFORMATION

- If you're looking for accommodation to rent, look out for:
  ZU VERMIETEN (for rent)
  APPARTEMENTS (apartments)
  FERIENWOHNUNGEN (holiday apartments)
  CHALETS
- For arranging details of your let, see 'Hotel' p. 26.
- Key words you will meet if renting on the spot:
  die Kaution   deposit
  de kow-tsee-*on*
  der Schlüssel   key
  der shlo*oss*el
- Having arranged your own accommodation and arrived with the key, check the obvious basics that you take for granted at home.
  Electricity: Voltage? Razors and small appliances brought from home may need adjusting. You may need an adaptor.
  Gas: Town gas or bottled gas? Butane gas must be kept indoors, propane gas must be kept outdoors.
  Stove: Don't be surprised to find:
  —the grill inside the oven, or no grill at all.
  —a lid covering the rings which lifts up to form a 'splashback'.
  —a mixture of two gas rings and two electric rings.
  Toilet: Main drainage or septic tank? Don't flush disposable diapers or anything else down the toilet if you are on a septic tank.
  Water: Find the stopcock. Check taps and plugs—they may not operate in the way you are used to. Check how to turn on (or light) the hot water.
  Windows: Check the method of opening and closing windows and shutters.
  Insects: Is an insecticide spray provided? If not, get one locally.
  Equipment: For buying or replacing equipment, see p. 54.
- You will probably have an official agent, but be clear in your own mind who to contact in an emergency, even if it is only a neighbour in the first place.

WHAT TO SAY

My name is ...	**Mein Name ist ...** mine nahmeh ist ...
I'm staying at ...	**Ich wohne im ...** ish voneh im ...
They've cut off ...	**Man hat ... abgestellt** man hat ... up-gashtellt
the electricity	**den Strom** den shtrome
the gas	**das Gas** das gahs
the water	**das Wasser** das vasser
Is there ... in the area?	**Gibt es ... in der Nähe?** geept es ... in der nay-eh
an electrician	**einen Elektriker** inen elek-trik-er
a plumber	**einen Klempner** inen klemp-ner
a gas fitter	**einen Installateur** inen in-stallah-ter
Where is ...	**Wo ist ...** vo ist ...
the fuse box?	**der Sicherungskasten?** der zisher-oongs-kasten
the stopcock?	**der Abstellhahn?** der up-shtell-hahn
the boiler?	**der Boiler?** der boy-ler
the water heater?	**der Warmwasserbereiter?** der vahm-vasser-beryter
Is there ...	**Gibt es hier ...** geept es here ...
town gas?	**Stadtgas?** shtatt-gahs
bottled gas?	**Flaschengas?** flashen-gahs
a septic tank?	**eine Sickergrube?** ineh zicker-groobeh
central heating?	**Zentralheizung?** tsentrahl-hy-tsoong
The cooker	**Der Herd** der hairt

The hair dryer	**Der Fön**
	der fern
The heating	**Die Heizung**
	dee hy-tsoong
The boiler	**Der Boiler**
	der boy-ler
The iron	**Das Bügeleisen**
	das boogel-izen
The pilot light	**Die Zündflamme**
	dee tsoont-flammeh
The refrigerator	**Der Kühlschrank**
	der kool-shrank
The telephone	**Das Telefon**
	das telefone
The toilet	**Die Toilette**
	dee twa-letteh
The washing machine	**Die Waschmaschine**
	dee vash-machine-eh
The water heater	**Der Warmwasserbereiter**
	der vahm-vasser-beryter
... is not working	**... funktioniert nicht**
	... foonk-tsee-o-neert nisht
Where can I get ...	**Wo kann ich ... bekommen?**
	vo kan ish ... bekommen
an adaptor for this?	**hierfür einen Zwischenstecker**
	here-foor inen tsvishen-shtecker
a bottle of butane gas?	**eine Flasche Butangas**
	ineh flasheh bootahn-gahs
a bottle of propane gas?	**eine Flasche Propangas**
	ineh flasheh bootahn-gahs
a fuse?	**eine Sicherung**
	ineh zisher-oong
an insecticide spray?	**ein Insektenspray**
	ine in-zekten-shpray
a light bulb?	**eine Glühbirne**
	ineh gloo-beerneh
The drain	**Der Abfluss**
	der up-flooss
The sink	**Der Ausguss**
	der ows-gooss
The toilet	**Die Toilette**
	dee twa-letteh
... is blocked	**... ist verstopft**
	.. ist fer-shtopft

The gas is leaking	**Die Gasleitung ist undicht** dee gahs-lite-oong ist oon-disht
Can you mend it straightaway?	**Können Sie es sofort reparieren?** kernnen zee es zofort repareeren
When can you mend it?	**Wann können Sie es reparieren?** vann kernnen zee es repareeren
How much do I owe you?	**Wieviel schulde ich Ihnen?** vee-feel shooldeh ish eenen
When is the rubbish collected?	**Wann kommt die Müllabfuhr?** vann komt dee mooll-up-foor

LIKELY REACTIONS

What's your name?	**Wie ist Ihr Name?** vee ist eer nahmeh
What's your address?	**Wie ist Ihre Adresse?** vee ist eereh adresseh
There's a shop ...	**Es gibt einen Laden ...** es geept inen lahden ...
in town	**in der Stadt** in der shtatt
in the village	**im Dorf** im dorf
I can't come ...	**Ich kann ... nicht kommen** ish kan ... nisht kommen
today	**heute** hoy-teh
this week	**diese Woche** deezeh vok-eh
I can't come until Monday	**Ich kann erst Montag kommen** ish kan erst mone-tahk kommen
I can come ...	**Ich kann ... kommen** ish kan ... kommen
on Tuesday	**Dienstag** deens-tahk
when you want	**jederzeit** yaider-tsyt
Every day	**Jeden Tag** yaiden tahk
Every other day	**Jeden zweiten Tag** yaiden tsvy-ten tahk
On Wednesdays [For days of the week, p. 133]	**Mittwochs** mitt-voks

General shopping

The drug store/The chemist's

**ESSENTIAL
INFORMATION**

- Look for the word
  APOTHEKE (drug store)
  or this sign:
- There are two kinds of
  drug store in Germany.
  The **APOTHEKE**
  (dispensing chemist's) is
  the place to go for
  prescriptions, medicines

  etc.; toilet and household articles, as well as patent medicines, are
  sold at the **DROGERIE** (chemist's shop).
- Try the drug store *before* going to a doctor: they are usually qualified
  to treat minor injuries.
- Drug stores are open during normal business hours, i.e. from 8.30
  a.m. to 12.30 p.m., and from 2.30 to 6.30 p.m. on weekdays. On
  Saturdays they close at 2.00 p.m.
- Drug stores take it in turns to stay open all night and on Sundays.
  If the drug store is shut, a notice on the door will give the address
  of the nearest night (**NACHTDIENST**) and Sunday service
  (**SONNTAGSDIENST**).
- Some toiletries can also be bought at a **PARFÜMERIE** but they will
  be more expensive.
- Finding a drug store, see p. 19.

WHAT TO SAY

I'd like . . .	**Ich möchte . . .**
	ish mershteh . . .
some Alka Seltzer	**Alka Seltzer**
	alka zeltser
some antiseptic	**ein antiseptisches Mittel**
	ine anti-zeptishes mittel

I'd like ...	Ich möchte ...
	ish mershteh ...
some aspirin	Aspirin
	ahs-pee-reen
some bandages	Verbandsstoff
	fer-bants-shtoff
some cotton wool	Watte
	vatteh
some eye drops	Augentropfen
	owghen-tropfen
some foot powder	Fusspuder
	fooss-pooder
some gauze dressing	Verbandmull
	fer-bant-mooll
some inhalant	ein Inhaliermittel
	ine in-hahleer-mittel
some insect repellent	ein Insektenschutzmittel
	ine in-zekten-shoots-mittel
some lip salve	eine Lippensalbe
	ineh lippen-zalbeh
some nose drops	Nasentropfen
	nahzen-tropfen
some sticking plaster	Heftpflaster
	heft-pflaster
some throat pastilles	Halspastillen
	hals-past-ill-en
some Vaseline	Vaseline
	vahzeh-leeneh
I'd like something for ...	Ich möchte etwas gegen ...
	ish mershteh etvas gay-ghen ...
bites (snakes, dogs)	Bisswunden
	bis-voon-den
burns	Verbrennungen
	fer-bren-oong-en
chilblains	Frostbeulen
	frost-boylen
a cold	Erkältung
	er-kelt-oong
constipation	Verstopfung
	fer-shtopf-oong
a cough	Husten
	hoosten

diarrhoea	**Durchfall**
	d*oo*rsh-fahl
ear-ache	**Ohrenschmerzen**
	*o*r-en-shmairts-en
flu	**Grippe**
	gr*i*ppeh
scalds	**Verbrühung**
	fer-br*oo*-oong
sore gums	**wundes Zahnfleisch**
	v*oo*ndes ts*a*hn-flysh
sprains	**Gelenkverstauchung**
	g*a*lenk-fer-shtow-koong
stings (mosquitos, bees)	**Insektenstiche**
	in-z*e*kten-shtee-sheh
sunburn	**Sonnenbrand**
	z*o*nnen-brant
car (air)/sea sickness	**Reisekrankheit/Seekrankheit**
	r*y*zeh-krank-hite/z*eh*-krank-hite
I need …	**Ich brauche …**
	ish br*ow*-keh …
some baby food	**Babynahrung**
	b*a*by-nah-roong
some contraceptives	**ein Verhütungsmittel**
	ine fer-h*oo*toongs-mittel
some deodorant	**einen Deodorant**
	*i*nen deo-dor*a*nt
some disposable nappies	**Papierwindeln**
	pap*ee*r-vin-deln
some handcream	**eine Handcreme**
	*i*neh h*a*nt-craym
some lipstick	**einen Lippenstift**
	*i*nen l*i*ppen-shtift
some make-up remover	**eine Reinigungsmilch**
	*i*neh ry-nee-goongs-milsh
some paper tissues	**Papiertücher**
	pap*ee*r-toosher
some razor blades	**Rasierklingen**
	raz*ee*r-kling-en
some safety pins	**Sicherheitsnadeln**
	z*i*sher-hyts-nahdeln
some sanitary towels	**Monatsbinden**
	m*o*nahts-bin-den

I need...	**Ich brauche**
	ish brow-keh ...
some shaving **cream**	**eine Rasiercreme**
	*i*neh razeer-craym
some soap	**ein Stück Seife**
	ine shtook z*y*-feh
some suntan lotion/oil	**Sonnenmilch/öl**
	*z*onnen-milsh/erl
some talcum powder	**Talkumpuder**
	t*a*l-koom-pooder
some Tampax	**eine Packung Tampax**
	*i*neh p*a*ck-oong t*a*mpax
some toilet paper	**Toilettenpapier**
	twa-*l*etten-papeer
some toothpaste	**eine Tube Zahnpasta**
	*i*neh t*oo*beh ts*a*hn-past*a*

[*For other essential expressions, see 'Shop talk', p. 57*]

Holiday items

ESSENTIAL INFORMATION

- Places to shop at and signs to look for:
  SCHREIBWARENGESCHÄFT (stationery)
  PHOTOGESCHÄFT (films)
  KUNSTGEWERBE (arts and crafts)
  GESCHENKARTIKEL (gifts)
- and the main department stores:
  KARSTADT
  HORTEN
  HERTIE
  KAUHOF

WHAT TO SAY

Where can I buy . . . ?	**Wo kann ich . . . kaufen?**
	vo kan ish . . . kow-fen
I'd like . . .	**Ich möchte . . .**
	ish mershteh
a bag	**eine Tasche**
	ineh tasheh
a beach ball	**einen Strandball**
	inen shtrant-bal
a bucket	**einen Eimer**
	inen imer
an English newspaper	**eine englische Zeitung**
	ineh eng-lisheh tsy-toong
some envelopes	**Briefumschläge**
	breef-oom-shlaig-eh
a guide book	**einen Reiseführer**
	inen ryzeh-foorer
a map (of the area)	**eine Landkarte von dieser Gegend**
	ineh lant-karteh fon deezer
	gay-ghent
some postcards	**Ansichtskarten**
	un-zishts-karten
a spade	**eine Schaufel**
	ineh sha-oofel
a straw hat	**einen Strohhut**
	inen shtro-hoot
a suitcase	**einen Koffer**
	inen koffer
some sunglasses	**eine Sonnenbrille**
	ineh zonnen-brilleh
a sunshade	**einen Sonnenschirm**
	inen zonnen-sheerm
an umbrella	**einen Regenschirm**
	inen ray-ghen-sheerm
some writing paper	**Schreibpapier**
	shripe-papeer
I'd like . . . [*show the camera*]	**Ich möchte . . .**
	ish mershteh ..
a colour film	**einen Farbfilm**
	inen farp-film
a black and white film	**einen Schwarzweiss-Film**
	inen shvarts-vice film

I'd like ... [*show the camera***]**   Ich möchte ...
    ish mershteh ...

  for prints   **für Abzüge**
    foor *u*p-tsoog-eh

  for slides   **für Dias**
    foor dee-ahs

  12 (24/36) exposures   **zwölf (vierundzwanzig/**
    sechsunddreissig) Aufnahmen
    tsverlf (f*ee*r-oont-tsvan-sik/
    z*e*x-oont-dry-sik) *o*wf-nahmen

  a standard 8mm film   **einen acht Millimeter Film**
    *i*nen ahkt m*i*lli-maiter film

  a super 8 film   **einen Super-Acht-Film**
    *i*nen z*oo*per ahkt film

  some flash bulbs   **Blitzlichter**
    bl*i*ts-lish-ter

This camera is broken   **Diese Kamera ist kaputt**
    d*ee*zeh kamera ist kah-p*oo*t

The film is stuck   **Der Film klemmt**
    der f*i*lm klemmt

Please can you ...   **Können Sie bitte ...**
    k*e*rnnen zee b*i*tteh

  develop/print this?   **diesen Film entwickeln/abziehen?**
    d*ee*zen film ent-v*i*ckeln/*u*p-tseen

  load the camera?   **den Film einlegen?**
    dehn film *i*ne-laygen

[*For other essential expressions, see 'Shop talk', p. 57***]**

The smoke shop

ESSENTIAL INFORMATION

- A smoke shop is called a **TABAKWAREN** or **ZIGARRENLADEN**.
- Large supermarkets and department stores often have their own 'smoke shops' on the premises, a kind of stall near the entrance or cash registers.
- The smoke shop is the only place where you can get tobacco, cigars, pipe utensils, flints etc., whereas cigarettes can be bought at a variety of places:
  at the **KIOSK**
  at most foodstores
  from the cigarette machine round the corner
  inside a café, bar or pub etc.
- To ask if there is a smoke shop near by, see p. 19.

WHAT TO SAY

A packet of cigarettes ...	**Eine Schachtel Zigaretten ...**
	*ineh sh*a*ktel tsee-gar*e*tten ...*
with filters	**mit Filter**
	*mit f*i*lter*
without filters	**ohne Filter**
	o-*neh f*i*lter*
king size	**extra lang**
	*extrah l*a*ng*
menthol	**mit Menthol**
	*mit men-t*o*le*
Those up there ...	**Die da oben ...**
	dee dah o-*ben ...*
on the right	**rechts**
	reshts
on the left	**links**
	links
These [*point*]	**Diese hier**
	*d*e*ezeh here*
Cigarettes, please	**Zigaretten, bitte**
	*tsee-gar*e*tten b*i*tteh*

100, 200, 300	**einhundert, zweihundert, dreihundert** _i_ne-hoondert tsvy-hoondert dry-hoondert
Two packets	**Zwei Schachteln** tsvy sh_a_kteln
Have you got ...	**Haben Sie ...** h_a_hben zee
English cigarettes?	**englische Zigaretten?** eng-lisheh tsee-garetten
American cigarettes?	**amerikanische Zigaretten?** ameri-k_a_h-nisheh tsee-garetten
English pipe tobacco?	**englischen Pfeifentabak?** eng-lishen pf_y_fen-tabak
American pipe tobacco?	**amerikanischen Pfeifentabak?** ameri-k_a_h-nishen pf_y_fen-tabak
rolling tobacco?	**Zigarettentabak?** tsee-garetten-tabak
A packet of pipe tobacco	**Eine Packung Pfeifentabak** _i_neh p_a_ck-oong pf_y_fen-tabak
That one down there ...	**Den da unten ...** dehn dah _oo_nten ...
on the right	**rechts** reshts
on the left	**links** links
This one [_point_]	**Diesen hier** d_ee_zen here
A cigar, please	**Eine Zigarre, bitte** _i_neh tsee-g_a_rreh b_i_tteh
That one [_point_]	**Die da** d_ee_ dah
Some cigars, please	**Zigarren, bitte** tsee-g_a_rren b_i_tteh
Those [_point_]	**Die da** d_ee_ dah
A box of matches	**Eine Schachtel Streichhölzer** _i_neh sh_a_ktel shtr_y_sh-herltser
A packet of pipe-cleaners	**Eine Packung Pfeifenreiniger** _i_neh p_a_ck-oong pf_y_fen-ry-neeg-er

A packet of flints	**Eine Packung Feuersteine**
[*show lighter*]	*i*neh pack-oong f*oy*-er-shtine-eh
Lighter fuel	**Feuerzeugbenzin**
	f*oy*-er-tsoyk-bentseen
Lighter gas, please	**Feuerzeuggass, bitte**
	f*oy*-er-tsoyk-gahs b*i*tteh

[*For other essential expressions, see 'Shop talk', p. 57*]

Buying clothes

ESSENTIAL INFORMATION

- Look for:
  DAMENBEKLEIDUNG (women's clothes)
  HERRENBEKLEIDUNG (men's clothes)
  SCHUHGESCHÄFT (shoe shop)
- Don't buy without being measured first or without trying things on.
- Don't rely on conversion charts of clothing sizes (see p. 144).
- If you are buying for someone else, take their measurements with you.
- All major department stores [*see p. 44*] sell clothes and shoes.

WHAT TO SAY

I'd like ...	**Ich möchte ...**
	ish mershteh ...
an anorak	**einen Anorak**
	*i*nen *a*h-norak
a belt	**einen Gürtel**
	*i*nen g*oo*r-tel
a bikini	**einen Bikini**
	*i*nen bik*i*ni
a bra	**einen Büstenhalter/BH**
	*i*nen b*oo*sten-halter/beh-h*ah*

I'd like ...	Ich möchte ... ish mershteh ...
a cap (swimming)	eine Badekappe *i*neh b*a*hdeh-kappeh
(skiing)	eine Skimütze *i*neh sh*ee*-mootseh
a cardigan	eine Wolljacke *i*neh v*o*ll-yackeh
a coat	einen Mantel *i*nen m*a*ntel
a dress	ein Kleid ine kl*i*te
a hat	einen Hut *i*nen hoot
a jacket	eine Jacke *i*neh yah-keh
a jumper	einen Pullover *i*nen pull-*o*ver
a nightdress	ein Nachthemd ine n*a*kt-hemt
a pullover	einen Pullover *i*nen pull-*o*ver
some pyjamas	einen Schlafanzug *i*nen shl*a*hf-un-tsook
a raincoat	einen Regenmantel *i*nen r*a*y-ghen-mantel
a shirt (women)	eine Bluse *i*neh bl*oo*zeh
a shirt (men)	ein Oberhemd ine *o*-ber-hemt
a skirt	einen Rock *i*nen rock
a suit (women)	ein Kostüm ine kost-*oo*m
a suit (men)	einen Anzug *i*nen *u*n-tsook
a swimsuit	einen Badeanzug *i*nen b*a*hdeh-un-tsook
some tights	eine Strumpfhose *i*neh shtr*oo*mpf-hozeh
some trousers	eine Hose *i*neh h*o*zeh

a T-shirt	**ein T-Shirt**
	ine *tee*-shirt
I'd like a pair of ...	**Ich möchte ein Paar ...**
	ish m*e*rshteh ine par ...
briefs (women)	**Damenschlüpfer**
	d*a*hmen-shloopfer
gloves	**Handschuhe**
	h*a*nt-shoo-eh
jeans	**Jeans**
	jeans
shorts	**Shorts**
	shorts
(short/long) socks	**(Kurze/lange) Socken**
	(k*oo*r-tseh/l*a*ngeh) z*o*cken
stockings	**Strümpfe**
	shtr*oo*m-feh
underpants (men)	**Herrenunterhosen**
	h*e*rren-*oo*nter-hozen
I'd like a pair of ...	**Ich möchte ein Paar ...**
	ish m*e*rshteh ine par
shoes	**Schuhe**
	sh*oo*-eh
canvas shoes	**Tennisschuhe**
	tennis-sh*oo*-eh
sandals	**Sandalen**
	zand*a*hlen
beach shoes	**Strandsandalen**
	shtr*a*nt-zand*a*hlen
smart shoes	**elegante Schuhe**
	ele-g*a*nteh sh*oo*eh
boots	**Stiefel**
	sht*ee*-fel
moccasins	**Mokassins**
	mok*a*ssins
My size is ...	**Ich habe Grösse ...**
	ish h*a*hbeh gr*e*rsseh ...

[*For numbers, see p. 129*]

Can you measure me, please?	**Können Sie bitte meine Masse nehmen?**
	k*e*rnnen zee b*i*tteh m*i*neh m*a*hsseh nay-men

Can I try it on?	**Kann ich es anprobieren?**
	kan ish es *un*-pro-beeren
It's for a present	**Es soll ein Geschenk sein**
	es zoll ine gash*e*nk zine
These are the measurements	**Hier sind die Masse**
[*show written*]	here zint dee m*a*hsseh
bust	**Oberweite**
	o-ber-vy-teh
chest	**Brustumfang**
	br*oo*st-oom-fang
collar	**Kragenweite**
	kr*a*h-ghen-vy-teh
hip	**Hüftumfang**
	h*oo*ft-oom-fang
leg	**Beinlänge**
	b*i*ne-leng-eh
waist	**Taillenweite**
	t*a*l-yen-vy-teh
Have you got something …	**Haben Sie etwas …**
	h*a*hben zee *e*tvas …
in black?	**in schwarz?**
	in shv*a*rts
in white?	**in weiss?**
	in v*i*ce
in grey?	**in grau?**
	in gr*a*-oo
in blue?	**in blau?**
	in bl*a*-oo
in brown?	**in braun?**
	in brown
in pink?	**in rosa?**
	in r*o*za
in green?	**in grün?**
	in gr*oo*n
in red?	**in rot?**
	in r*o*te
in yellow?	**in gelb?**
	in gh*e*lp
in this colour? [*point*]	**in dieser Farbe?**
	in d*ee*zer farbeh
in cotton?	**in Baumwolle?**
	in b*ow*m-volleh

in denim?	**in Jeansstoff?**
	in jeans-shtoff
in leather?	**in Leder?**
	in lay-der
in nylon?	**in Nylon?**
	in nylon
in suede?	**in Wildleder?**
	in vilt-lay-der
in wool?	**in Wolle?**
	in volleh
in this material? [*point*]	**in diesem Material?**
	in deezem materi-ahl

[*For other essential expressions, see 'Shop talk', p. 57*]

Replacing equipment

ESSENTIAL INFORMATION

- Look for these shops and signs:
  EISENWARENHANDLUNG (hardware)
  HAUSHALTSWAREN (household goods)
  ELEKTROGESCHÄFT (electrical goods)
  DROGERIE (household cleaning materials)
- In a supermarket, look for this display:
  HAUSHALTSARTIKEL
- To ask the way to the shop, see p. 19.
- At a campsite try their shop first.

WHAT TO SAY

Have you got . . .	Haben Sie . . .
	hahben zee . . .
an adaptor? [*show appliance*]	**einen Zwischenstecker?**
	*i*nen tsv*i*shen-shtecker
a bottle of butane gas?	**eine Flasche Butangas?**
	*i*neh fl*a*sheh boot*a*hn-gahs
a bottle of propane gas?	**eine Flasche Propangas?**
	*i*neh fl*a*sheh pro-p*a*hn-gahs
a bottle opener?	**einen Flaschenöffner?**
	*i*nen fl*a*shen-erffner
a corkscrew?	**einen Korkenzieher?**
	*i*nen k*o*rken-tsee-er
any disinfectant?	**ein Desinfektionsmittel?**
	ine des-infek-tsee-*o*ns-mittel
any disposable cups?	**Pappbecher?**
	p*a*p-besher
any disposable plates?	**Pappteller?**
	p*a*p-teller
a drying up cloth?	**ein Geschirrtuch?**
	ine gash*ee*r-took
any forks?	**Gabeln?**
	g*a*h-beln
a fuse? [*show old one*]	**eine Sicherung?**
	*i*neh z*i*sher-oong

an insecticide spray?	ein Insektenspray?
	*i*ne in-*zek*ten-shpray
a paper kitchen roll?	eine Rolle Küchenpapier?
	*i*neh *r*olleh k*oo*-shen-pap*ee*r
any knives?	Messer?
	*m*esser
a light bulb [*show old one*]	eine Glühbirne?
	*i*neh gl*oo*-beer-neh
a plastic bucket?	einen Plastikeimer?
	*i*nen pl*a*stik-*i*mer
a plastic can?	einen Plastikkanister?
	*i*nen pl*a*stik-kan*i*ster
a scouring pad?	einen Topfkratzer?
	*i*nen *t*opf-kratser
a spanner?	einen Schraubenschlüssel?
	*i*nen shr*ow*ben-shl*oo*ssel
a sponge?	einen Schwamm?
	*i*nen shv*a*mm
any string?	Bindfaden?
	b*i*nt-fahden
any tent pegs?	Heringe fürs Zelt?
	h*e*ring-eh foors ts*e*lt
a tin opener?	einen Dosenöffner?
	*i*nen d*o*ze-en-erffner
a torch?	eine Taschenlampe?
	*i*neh t*a*shen-lampeh
any torch batteries?	Taschenlampenbatterien?
	t*a*shen-lampen-batter-*ee*-en
a universal plug (for the sink)?	einen Stöpsel (für das Spülbecken)?
	*i*nen sht*e*rp-zel foor das shp*oo*l-becken
a washing line?	eine Wäscheleine?
	*i*neh v*e*sheh-line-eh
any washing powder?	Waschpulver?
	v*a*sh-poolver
a washing-up brush?	eine Spülbürste?
	*i*neh shp*oo*l-boorsteh
any washing-up liquid?	ein Spülmittel?
	*i*ne shp*oo*l-mittel

[*For other essential expressions, see 'Shop talk', p. 57*]

Shop talk

ESSENTIAL INFORMATION

● Know your coins and bills.
German coins: see illustration.
German bills: 5, 10, 20, 50, 100 Deutschmark
Austrian coins: 1, 2, 5, 10, 20, 50 Groschen; 1, 5, 10 Schilling
Austrian bills: 20, 50, 100, 500 Schilling
Swiss coins: 5, 10, 20, 50 Rappen; 1, 2, 5 Franken
Swiss bills: 10, 20, 50, 100 Franken
● Know how to say the important weights and measures. Note that
though Germany is metric, people still use the word **Pfund** (pound).

50 grams	**fünfzig Gramm**
	*f*oonf-tsik gr*a*mm
100 grams	**einhundert Gramm**
	*i*ne-hoondert gramm
200 grams	**zweihundert Gramm**
	tsv*y*-hoondert gr*a*mm
½ lb (250 grams)	**ein halbes Pfund**
	*i*ne h*a*lbes pfoont
1 lb	**ein Pfund**
	*i*ne pfoont
1 kilo	**ein Kilo**
	*i*ne k*i*lo
2 kilos	**zwei Kilo**
	tsv*y* k*i*lo
½ litre	**einen halben Liter**
	*i*nen h*a*lben l*i*tre
1 litre	**einen Liter**
	*i*nen l*i*tre
2 litres	**zwei Liter**
[*For numbers, see p. 129*]	tsv*y* l*i*tre

● In small shops don't be surprised if customers, as well as the
shop asistant, say 'hello' and 'good-bye' to you.

CUSTOMER

Hello	**Guten Tag**
	goo-ten tahk
Hello (Austria)	**Grüss Gott**
	grooss got
Good morning	**Guten Morgen**
	goo-ten morgen
Good afternoon	**Guten Tag**
	goo-ten tahk
Good-bye	**Auf Wiedersehn**
	owf veeder-zain
I'm just looking	**Ich sehe mich nur um**
	ish zay-eh mish noor oom
Excuse me	**Entschuldigen Sie**
	ent-shool-dig-en zee
How much is this/that?	**Wieviel kostet dies/das?**
	vee-feel kostet dees/das
What is that? /What are those?	**Was ist das?**
	vas ist das
Is there a discount?	**Gibt es einen Rabatt?**
	geept es inen rah-batt
I'd like that, please	**Ich möchte das da, bitte**
	ish mershteh das dah bitteh
Not that	**Nicht das**
	nisht das
Like that	**Wie das da**
	vee das dah
That's enough, thank you	**Das ist genug, danke**
	das ist ganook dankeh
More please	**Mehr, bitte**
	mair bitteh
Less than that	**Etwas weniger**
	etvas vay-neeg-er
That's fine	**Das ist gut so**
	das ist goot zo
OK	**Gut**
	goot
I won't take it, thank you	**Ich nehme es nicht, danke**
	ish nay-meh es nisht dankeh
It's not right	**Es ist nicht das Richtige**
	es ist nisht das rish-teeg-eh

Thank you very much	**Vielen Dank**
	fee-len d*a*nk
Have you got something ...	**Haben Sie etwas ...**
	h*a*hben zee *e*tvas
better?	**Besseres?**
	b*e*sser-es
cheaper?	**Billigeres?**
	b*i*llig-er-es
different?	**anderes?**
	*a*nder-es
larger?	**Grösseres?**
	gr*e*rsser-es
smaller?	**Kleineres?**
	kl*i*ner-es
At what time do you ...	**Um wieviel Uhr ...**
	oom v*ee*-feel *oo*r ...
open?	**öffnen Sie?**
	*e*rffnen zee
close?	**schliessen Sie?**
	shl*ee*ssen zee
Can I have a bag, please?	**Kann ich bitte eine Tragetasche haben?**
	kan ish b*i*tteh *i*neh tr*a*hg-eh-tasheh h*a*hben
Can I have a receipt?	**Kann ich eine Quittung haben?**
	kan ish *i*neh kv*i*tt-oong h*a*hben
Do you take ...	**Nehmen Sie ...**
	n*ay*-men zee ...
English/American money?	**englisches/amerikanisches Geld?**
	*e*ng-lishes/ameri-k*a*h-nishes ghelt
travellers' cheques?	**Reiseschecks?**
	r*y*zeh-shecks
credit cards?	**Kreditkarten?**
	kred*ee*t-karten
I'd like ...	**Ich möchte ...**
	ish m*e*rshteh ...
one like that	**eins davon**
	*i*nes d*a*h-fon
two like that	**zwei davon**
	tsvy d*a*h-fon

SHOP ASSISTANT

Can I help you?	**Kann ich Ihnen behilflich sein?** kan ish *ee*nen beh*i*lf-lish z*i*ne
What would you like?	**Was darf es sein** vas darf es z*i*ne
Will that be all?	**Kommt noch etwas dazu?** komt nok *e*tvas dah-ts*oo*
Is that all?	**Ist das alles?** ist das *a*lles
Anything else?	**Sonst noch etwas?** z*o*nst nok *e*tvas
Would you like it wrapped?	**Soll ich es einwickeln?** zoll ish es *i*ne-vickeln
Sorry, none left	**Leider ausverkauft** l*i*der *o*ws-fer-kowft
I haven't got any	**Wir haben keine** veer h*a*hben k*i*neh
I haven't got any more	**Wir haben keine mehr** veer h*a*hben k*i*neh mair
How many do you want?	**Wieviele möchten Sie?** v*ee*-feeleh m*e*rshten z*ee*
How much do you want?	**Wieviel möchten Sie?** v*ee*-feel m*e*rshten z*ee*
Is that enough?	**Ist das genug?** ist das gan*oo*k

Shopping for food

Bread

ESSENTIAL INFORMATION

- Finding a baker's, see p. 19.
- Key words to look for:
  BÄCKEREI (baker's)
  BÄCKER (baker)
  BROT (bread)
- Supermarkets of any size and general stores nearly always sell bread.
- Bakers are open from 7.30 a.m. to 12.30 p.m. and from 2.30 to 6.30 p.m. on weekdays. On Saturdays they close at lunchtime. Many bakers will open on Sunday mornings from 10 a.m. to noon and close one afternoon during the week, usually on Wednesdays.

WHAT TO SAY

Some bread, please	**Brot, bitte** brote bitteh
A loaf (like that)	**Ein Brot (wie das da)** ine brote (vee das dah)
A large one	**Ein grosses** ine grosses
A small one	**Ein kleines** ine kline-es
A bread roll	**Ein Brötchen** ine brert-shen
A bread roll (Bavaria, Austria)	**Eine Semmel** ineh zemmel
A crescent roll	**Ein Hörnchen** ine hern-shen
Bread	**Brot** brote
Sliced bread	**Geschnittenes Brot** ga-shnitten-es brote

White bread	**Weissbrot**
	vice-brote
Rye bread	**Graubrot**
	gra-oo-brote
(Black) rye bread	**Schwarzbrot**
	shvarts-brote
Wholemeal bread	**Vollkornbrot**
	foll-korn-brote
Two loaves	**Zwei Brote**
	tsvy brote-eh
Four bread rolls	**Vier Brötchen**
	feer brert-shen
Four crescent rolls	**Vier Hörnchen**
	feer hern-shen

[*For other essential expressions, see 'Shop talk', p. 57*]

Cakes

ESSENTIAL INFORMATION

- Key words to look for:
  BÄCKEREI (bread and cake shop)
  KONDITOREI (cake shop, often with a tea-room in the back)
- To find a cake shop, see p. 19.
- **CAFÉ** or **KAFFEEHAUS** in Austria: a place to buy cakes and have a drink at a table, usually in the afternoon. See also p. 80, 'Ordering a drink'.

WHAT TO SAY

The type of cakes you find in the shops varies slightly from region to region but the following are some of the most common.

der Berliner	jam filled doughnut
der ber-leener	
der Florentiner	almond flakes on a thin cake and
der flor-en-teener	chocolate base

die Schwarzwälder Kirschtorte dee shvarts-velder keersh-torteh	Black Forest cake
die Obsttorte dee obst-torteh	fruit on a sponge base with glazing over
der Apfelstrudel der apfel-shtroodel	flaky pastry filled with apple, nuts, and raisins
der Mohrenkopf der moren-kopf	ball-shaped pastry filled with pudding, covered with chocolate
der Käsekuchen der kaizeh-kooken	cheesecake
die Sachertorte dee zahker-torteh	rich Viennese chocolate cake with jam
der Sandkuchen der zant-kooken	Madeira cake
die Sahnetorte dee zah-neh-torteh	cream cake
der Bienenstich der beenen-shtish	cream cake sprinkled with flaky almonds and honey

You usually buy individual pastries by number:

Two doughnuts, please	**Zwei Berliner, bitte** tsvy ber-leener bitteh

You buy large cakes by the slice:

One slice of fruit tart	**Ein Stück Obsttorte** ine shtook obst-torteh
Two slices of Madeira cake	**Zwei Stück Sandkuchen** tsvy shtook zant-kooken

You may also want to say:

With whipped cream, please	**Mit Sahne, bitte** mit zah-neh bitteh

[*For other essential expressions, see 'Shop talk', p. 57*]

Ice-cream and sweets

ESSENTIAL INFORMATION

- Key words to look for:
  EIS (ice-cream)
  EISDIELE (ice-cream parlour)
  EISCAFÉ (ice-cream parlour/tea room)
  SÜSSWARENLADEN (sweet shop)
  KONDITOREI (cake shop)
- Best known ice-cream brand names:
  LANGNESE   **SCHÖLLER**
  DR OETKER   **JOPA**
- Pre-packed sweets are available in general stores and supermarkets.

WHAT TO SAY

A . . . ice, please...	**Ein . . . -Eis, bitte** *ine . . . ice bitteh*
strawberry	**Erdbeer** *airt-bear*
chocolate	**Schokoladen** *shoko-lahden*
vanilla	**Vanille** *vanilyeh*
lemon	**Zitronen** *tsee-tronen*
caramel	**Karamel** *kara-mel*
raspberry	**Himbeer** *him-bear*
At the table	
A single portion	**Eine kleine Portion** *ineh kly-neh por-tsee-on*
Two single portions	**Zwei kleine Portionen** *tsvy kly-neh por-tsee-onen*
A double portion	**Eine grosse Portion** *ineh grosseh por-tsee-on*

Two double portions	**Zwei grosse Portionen**
	tsvy grosseh por-tsee-onen
A mixed ice ...	**Ein gemischtes Eis ...**
	ine ga-mishtes ice ...
with/without whipped cream	mit/ohne Sahne
	mit/ohneh zahneh

Over the counter

A cone ...	**Ein Hörnchen ...**
	ine hern-shen ...
A tub ...	**Einen Becher ...**
	inen besher ...
with two scoops	mit zwei Kugeln
	mit tsvy koog-eln
with three scoops	mit drei Kugeln
	mit dry koog-eln
(60 Pfennig's) worth of ice-cream	**Ein Eis zu (sechzig)**
	ine ice tsoo (zek-tsig)
A packet of ...	**Eine Packung ...**
	ineh pack-oong ...
100 grams of ...	**Hundert Gramm ...**
	hoondert gramm ...
200 grams of ...	**Zweihundert Gramm ...**
	tsvy-hoondert gramm ...
sweets	**Bonbons**
	bong-bongs
toffees	**Karamelbonbons**
	karamel-bong-bongs
chocolates	**Pralinen**
	pra-leenen
mints	**Pfefferminzbonbons**
	pfeffer-mints-bong-bongs
A lollipop	**Einen Dauerlutscher**
	inen dower-lootsher

[For other essential expressions, see 'Shop talk', p. 57]

In the supermarket

ESSENTIAL INFORMATION

- The place to ask for: [*see p. 19*]
  EIN SUPERMARKT
  EIN SELBSTBEDIENUNGSLADEN (corner self-service)
  EIN LEBENSMITTELGESCHÄFT (general food store)
- Key instructions on signs in the shop:
  EINGANG (entrance)
  KEIN EINGANG (no entry)
  AUSGANG (exit)
  KEIN AUSGANG (no exit)
  KASSE (check-out, cash desk)
  SCHNELLKASSE (check-out for up to five items)
  IM ANGEBOT (on offer)
  SONDERANGEBOT (special offer)
  SELBSTBEDIENUNG (self-service)
- Large supermarkets are open all day from 8.00 a.m. to 6.30 p.m. The smaller corner shops usually close at lunchtime, from 12.30 to 2.30 p.m.
- For non-food items, see 'Replacing equipment', p. 54.
- No need to say anything in a supermarket, but ask if you can't see what you want.

WHAT TO SAY

Excuse me, please	**Entschuldigen Sie, bitte** ent-sh*oo*l-dig-en zee b*i*tteh
Where is ...	**Wo ist ...** v*o* ist ...
the bread?	**das Brot?** das br*o*te
the butter?	**die Butter?** dee b*oo*tter
the cheese?	**der Käse?** der k*ay*-zeh
the chocolate?	**die Schokolade?** dee shoko-l*a*hdeh

the coffee?	der Kaffee?
	der k*a*ffeh
the cooking oil?	das Speiseöl?
	das shp*i*zeh-erl
the fresh fish section?	die Fischabteilung?
	dee f*i*sh-abt*i*le-oong
the fruit?	das Obst?
	das *o*bst
the jam?	die Marmelade?
	dee marmeh-l*a*hdeh
the meat?	das Fleisch?
	das fl*y*sh
the milk?	die Milch?
	dee m*i*lsh
the mineral water	das Mineralwasser?
	das miner*a*hl-vasser
the salt?	das Salz?
	das z*a*lts
the sugar?	der Zucker?
	der ts*oo*cker
the tea?	der Tee?
	der t*a*y
the vegetable section?	die Gemüseabteilung?
	dee gam*oo*zeh-abt*i*loong
the vinegar?	der Essig?
	der *e*ssik
the wine?	der Wein?
	der v*i*ne
the yoghurt?	der Joghurt?
	der y*o*g-oort
Where are ...	**Wo sind ...**
	v*o* zint ...
the biscuits?	die Kekse?
	dee c*a*ke-seh
the crisps?	die Kartoffelchips?
	dee kar-t*o*ffel-ships
the eggs?	die Eier?
	dee *eye*-er
the frozen foods?	die Tiefkühlwaren?
	dee t*ee*f-kool-vahren
the fruit juices?	die Fruchtsäfte?
	dee fr*oo*kt-zefteh

Where are ...	Wo sind ... *vo* zint ...
the pastas?	die Teigwaren? dee *ti*ke-vahren
the soft drinks?	die alkoholfreien Getränke? dee alkoho*l*-fry-en gatr*e*nkeh
the sweets?	die Süssigkeiten? dee *zoo*-sick-kiten
the tinned vegetables?	die Gemüsekonserven? dee ga-m*oo*zeh-kon-zairven
the tinned foods?	die Konserven? dee kon-z*ai*rven

[For other essential expressions, see 'Shop talk', p. 57]

Picnic food

ESSENTIAL INFORMATION

- Key words to look for:
  DELIKATESSENGESCHÄFT ⎤
  FEINKOSTGESCHÄFT   ⎦ (delicatessen)
  METZGEREI ⎤
  SCHLACHTEREI ⎦ (butcher's)
- Weight guide:
  4-6 oz/150 g of prepared salad per two people, if eaten as a starter to a substantial meal.
  3-4 oz/100 g of prepared salad per person, if to be eaten as the main part of a picnic-type meal.

WHAT TO SAY

One slice of ...	Eine Scheibe ... *i*neh shy-beh ...
Two slices of ...	Zwei Scheiben ... tsvy shy-ben ...
roast beef	Rostbraten *r*ost-brahten

tongue sausage	**Zungenwurst**
	ts*oo*ngen-voorst
Saveloy sausage	**Zervelatwurst**
	zervel*a*ht-voorst
raw cured ham	**rohen Schinken**
	r*o*-en sh*i*nken
cooked ham	**gekochten Schinken**
	gak*o*kten sh*i*nken
garlic sausage	**Knoblauchwurst**
	kn*o*p-lowk-voorst
salami	**Salami**
	zal*a*h-mi
100 grams of ...	**Hundert Gramm ...**
	hoondert gramm ...
150 grams of ...	**Hundertfünfzig Gramm ...**
	hoondert-f*oo*nf-tsick gram ...
200 grams of ...	**Zweihundert Gramm ...**
	tsv*y*-hoondert gram ...
300 grams of ...	**Dreihundert Gramm ...**
	dr*y*-hoondert gram ...
herring salad	**Heringsalat**
	h*e*ring-zalaht
egg and mayonnaise salad	**Eiersalat**
	*ey*e-er-zalaht
chicken salad	**Geflügelsalat**
	gafl*oo*g-el-zalaht
tomato salad	**Tomatensalat**
	tom*a*hten-zalaht
potato salad	**Kartoffelsalat**
	kart*o*ffel-zalaht

You might also like to try some of these:

eine Pizza	a pizza
*i*neh p*i*zza	
ein Stück Gänseleberpastete	some goose liver pâté
*i*ne shtook	
ghen-zeh-laber-past*ai*teh	
ein Stück Fleischwurst	some luncheon sausage
*i*ne shtook fl*y*sh-voorst	
einen Matjeshering	white salted herring
*i*nen m*a*t-yes-hering	

eine Frikadelle	a spicy thick hamburger
*i*neh frikah-d*e*lleh	(often eaten cold)
einen Räucheraal	a smoked eel
*i*nen r*o*y-sher-ahl	
ein paar Frankfurter	two Frankfurter sausages
ine par fr*a*nk-f*oo*rter	
eine Weisswurst	a Bavarian sausage
*i*neh v*i*ce-voorst	
eine Thüringer Bratwurst	a spicy sausage from Thuringia
*i*neh t*oo*ring-er br*a*ht-voorst	
einen Elsässer Wurstsalat	shredded meat and cheese salad
*i*nen *e*l-zesser v*o*orst-zal*a*ht	
ein Stück Leberkäse	some meatloaf
ine shtook *l*aber-kay-zeh	
eine Wurstpastete	a sausage roll
*i*neh v*o*orst-past*a*iteh	
eine Königin-Pastete	a vol-au-vent
*i*neh k*e*rneeg-in past*a*iteh	
eine Geflügelpastete	a chicken vol-au-vent
*i*neh gafl*oo*g-el-past*a*iteh	
einen Kräuterquark	soft cream cheese with herbs
*i*nen kr*o*yter-kwark	
Tilsiter	mild cheese
t*i*l-zit-er	
Kümmelkäse	cheese with caraway seeds
k*oo*mmel-kaizeh	
einen Harzer Roller	sharp roll-shaped cheese
*i*nen h*a*rtser r*o*ller	
Emmentaler	Swiss cheese
*e*mmen-tahler	
Gouda	Dutch cheese
g*o*wdah	
Camembert/Brie	Camembert/Brie
c*a*men-bair/br*ee*	

[*For other essential expressions, see 'Shop talk', p. 57*]

Fruit and vegetables

ESSENTIAL INFORMATION

- Key words to look for:
  OBST (fruit)
  GEMÜSE (vegetables)
  OBST- UND GEMÜSEHÄNDLER (greengrocer)
- If possible, buy fruit and vegetables in the market where they are cheaper and fresher than in the shops.
- Weight guide:
  1 kilo of potatoes is sufficient for six people for one meal.

WHAT TO SAY

1lb ($\frac{1}{2}$ kilo) of ...	**Ein Pfund (ein halbes Kilo) ...**
	ine pfoont (ine halbes kilo) ...
1 kilo of ...	**Ein Kilo ...**
	ine kilo ...
2 kilos of ...	**Zwei Kilo ...**
	tsvy kilo ...
apples	**Äpfel**
	epfel
bananas	**Bananen**
	banah-nen
cherries	**Kirschen**
	keer-shen
grapes	**Weintrauben**
	vine-tra-ooben
oranges	**Apfelsinen**
	apfel-zeenen
pears	**Birnen**
	beer-nen
peaches	**Pfirsiche**
	pfeer-zisheh
plums	**Pflaumen**
	pfla-oomen
strawberries	**Erdbeeren**
	aird-bairen
A pineapple, please	**Eine Ananas, bitte**
	ineh ah-nanas bitteh

A grapefruit	**Eine Pampelmuse**
	*i*neh pampel-m*oo*zeh
A melon	**Eine Melone**
	*i*neh melone-eh
A water melon	**Eine Wassermelone**
	*i*neh *va*sser-melone-eh
½lb of ...	**Ein halbes Pfund ...**
	*i*ne h*a*lbes pfoont
1lb of ...	**Ein Pfund ...**
	*i*ne pfoont ...
1 kilo of ...	**Ein Kilo ...**
	*i*ne k*i*lo ...
3lbs of ...	**Drei Pfund ...**
	dr*y* pfoont ...
2 kilos of ...	**Zwei Kilo ...**
	tsv*y* k*i*lo ...
artichokes	**Artischocken**
	arti-sh*o*ken
aubergines	**Auberginen**
	ober-g*ee*nen
avocado pears	**Avokados**
	ahvo-k*ah*dos
carrots	**Karotten**
	kar*o*tten
courgettes	**Zucchini**
	tsoo-k*i*ni
green beans	**grüne Bohnen**
	gr*oo*neh b*o*ne-en
leeks	**Lauch/Porree**
	lowk/p*o*r-ray
mushrooms	**Pilze**
	p*i*l-tseh
onions	**Zwiebeln**
	tsv*ee*-beln
peas	**Erbsen**
	*ai*rpsen
potatoes	**Kartoffeln**
	kar-t*o*ffeln
red cabbage	**Rotkohl**
	r*o*te-kole
spinach	**Spinat**
	shpee-n*ah*t
tomatoes	**Tomaten**
	tom*a*hten

A bunch of …	Ein Bund …
	*i*ne boont …
parsley	**Petersilie**
	pater-*zeel*-yeh
radishes	**Radieschen**
	rah-*dees*-shen
shallots	**Schalotten**
	shah-*lott*en
A head of garlic	**Knoblauch**
	kn*o*pe-la-ook
A lettuce	**Einen Kopfsalat**
	*i*nen k*o*pf-zalaht
A cauliflower	**Einen Blumenkohl**
	*i*nen bl*oo*men-kole
A cabbage	**Einen Weisskohl**
	*i*nen v*i*ce-kole
A cucumber	**Eine Salatgurke**
	*i*neh zal*a*ht-goorkeh
Like that, please	**So eine, bitte**
	zo *i*neh b*i*tteh

Here are some fruit and vegetables which may not be familiar:

Zwetschgen	type of plum used for plum tart
tsv*e*tsh-gen	
Sauerkirsche	small sour-tasting variety of
z*o*w-er-keersheh	cherry
Reneklode	small yellow plum
reneh-kl*o*deh	
Mandarine	mandarin orange
mandah-*ree*neh	
Klementine	pipless, small tangerine
klemen-t*ee*neh	
Kohlrabi	vegetable similar to turnip in
kole-r*a*hbee	shape and taste
Fenchel	fennel, crunchy vegetable with
f*e*nshel	aniseed flavour
Wirsingkohl	Savoy, variety of cabbage
v*ee*r-zing-kole	

[*For other essential expressions, see 'Shop talk', p. 57*]

Beef Rind

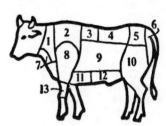

1 Hals
2 Zungenstück Zungengrat
3 Hohe Rippe
4 Filet (Lende)
5 Hüfte
6 Schwanzstück
7 Stich
8 Schulter
9 Querrippe (Zwerchrippe)
10 Blume (Rose)
11 Brust
12 Bauch (Nabel)
13 Beinfleisch

Veal Kalb

1 Hals
2 Nacken
3 Kotelett
4 Nierenbraten
5 Keule (Schlegel)
6 Blatt
7 Brust
8 Schulter
9 Haxe

Pork Schwein

1 Keule
2 Rücken
3 Nacken (Kamm)
4 Bauch
5 Schulter (Vorderschinken)
6 Eisbein

Mutton Hammel

1 Keule
2 Rücken
3 Hals
4 Brust
5 Schulter

Meat

ESSENTIAL INFORMATION

- Key words to look for:

| METZGEREI
FLEISCHEREI
SCHLACHTEREI | (butcher's) | METZGER
FLEISCHER
SCHLACHTER | (butcher) |

- Weight guide: 4-6 oz/125-200 g of meat per person for one meal.
- The diagrams opposite are to help you make sense of labels on counters and supermarket displays, and decide which cut or joint to have. Translations do not help, and you don't need to say the German word involved.
- You will find that lamb and especially mutton are less popular in Germany. The butcher's display will tell you what's available.

WHAT TO SAY

For a joint, choose the type of meat and then say how many people it is for:

Some beef, please	**Rindfleisch, bitte** rint-flysh bitteh
Some lamb	**Lamm** lamm
Some mutton	**Hammelfleisch** hammel-flysh
Some pork	**Schweinefleisch** shvine-eh-flysh
Some veal	**Kalbfleisch** kalp-flysh
A joint ...	**Einen Braten ...** inen brahten ...
for two people	**für zwei Personen** foor tsvy per-zonen
for four people	**für vier Personen** foor feer per-zonen

For steak, liver or kidneys, do as above:

Some steak, please	**Steak, bitte**
	st*eak* b*i*tte
Some liver	**Leber**
	l*a*ber
Some kidneys	**Nieren**
	n*ee*ren
Some sausages	**Würstchen**
	v*oo*rst-shen
Some minced meat	**Hackfleisch**
	h*a*ck-flysh
for three people	**für drei Personen**
	foor dr*y* per-z*o*nen
for five people	**für fünf Personen**
	foor f*oo*nf per-z*o*nen

For chops, do it this way:

Two veal escalopes, please	**Zwei Kalbsschnitzel, bitte**
	tsv*y* k*a*lps-shnitsel b*i*tteh
Three pork chops	**Drei Schweinekoteletts**
	dr*y* shv*i*ne-eh-kotlets
Five lamb chops	**Fünf Lammkoteletts**
	f*oo*nf l*a*mm-kotlets

You may also want:

A chicken	**Ein Huhn**
	ine hoon
A tongue	**Eine Zunge**
	*i*neh ts*oo*ng-eh

Other essential expressions [*see also p. 57*]:

Please can you ...	**Können Sie ... bitte?**
	kernnen zee ... b*i*tteh
mince it?	**es durch den Fleischwolf drehen**
	es doorsh den fl*y*sh-volf dr*ay*-en
dice it?	**es in kleine Stücke schneiden**
	es in kl*y*-neh sht*oo*ck-eh shn*y*den
trim the fat?	**das Fett abschneiden**
	das f*e*tt *u*p-shnyden

Fish

ESSENTIAL INFORMATION

- The place to ask for: **EIN FISCHGESCHÄFT** (fish shop) or the **FISCHABTEILUNG** (fish section) in the food departments of larger stores.
- Look out also for **NORDSEE** – a fish shop chain selling fresh fish and smoked and marinated specialities as well as snack meals.
- Shellfish (**MEERESFRÜCHTE**) is quite rare in Germany.
- Large markets usually have fresh fish stalls.
- Weight guide: 8 oz/250 g minimum per person, for one meal of fish bought on the bone.
  - i.e. ½ kilo/500 g   for two people
  - 1 kilo   for four people
  - 1½ kilos   for six people

WHAT TO SAY

Purchase large fish and small shellfish by the weight:

1lb (½ kilo) of …	**Ein Pfund …**
	ine pfoont …
1 kilo of …	**Ein Kilo …**
	ine k*i*lo …
3lbs (1½ kilos) of …	**Drei Pfund …**
	dr*y* pfoont …
cod	**Kabeljau**
	k*a*hbel-yow
haddock	**Schellfisch**
	shell-fish
turbot	**Steinbutt**
	sht*i*ne-boott
carp	**Karpfen**
	k*a*rp-fen
red sea-bass	**Rotbarsch**
	rote-barsh
halibut	**Heilbutt**
	h*i*le-boott

3lbs (1½ kilos) of ...	**Drei Pfund ...** dry pfoont ...
pike	**Hecht** hesht
shrimps	**Garnelen** gar-*nay*-len
shrimps (N. Germany)	**Granat** grah-*naht*
prawns	**Krabben** kr*a*bben
mussels	**Muscheln** m*oo*sheln

Some large fish can be purchased by the slice:

One slice of ...	**Ein Stück ...** *i*ne shtook ...
Two slices of ...	**Zwei Stück ...** tsv*y* shtook ...
Six slices of ...	**Sechs Stück ...** z*ex* shtook ...
cod	**Kabeljau** k*a*hbel-yow
haddock	**Schellfisch** sh*e*ll-fish
halibut	**Heilbutt** h*i*le-boott
Two slices of salmon	**Zwei Scheiben Lachs** tsv*y* sh*y*-ben laks

For some shellfish and 'frying pan' fish, specify the number you want:

A crab, please	**Einen Krebs, bitte** *i*nen kreps b*i*tteh
A lobster	**Einen Hummer** *i*nen h*oo*mmer
A spiny lobster	**Eine Languste** *i*neh lang*oo*st-eh
A plaice	**Eine Scholle** *i*neh sh*o*ll-eh
A trout	**Eine Forelle** *i*neh for*e*ll-eh

A sole	**Eine Seezunge**
	*i*neh *zay*-tsoong-eh
A mackerel	**Eine Makrele**
	*i*neh mak-r*ai*leh
A herring	**Einen Hering**
	*i*nen h*ai*r-ing

Other essential expressions [*see also p. 57*]:

Please can you ...	**Können Sie, bitte ...**
	k*e*rnnen zee b*i*tteh ...
take the heads off?	**Kopf und Schwanz entfernen?**
	k*o*pf oont shv*a*nts ent-f*ai*rnen
clean them?	**den Fisch ausnehmen?**
	den fish *o*ws-nay-men
fillet them?	**den Fisch in Scheiben schneiden?**
	den fish in sh*y*-ben shn*y*-den

Eating and drinking out

Ordering a drink

ESSENTIAL INFORMATION

- The places to ask for: **EIN CAFÉ** [see p. 19].
  EINE WIRTSCHAFT (a type of pub).
  EINE WEINSTUBE (a wine bar).
- By law, the price list of drinks (**GETRÄNKEKARTE**) must
  be displayed outside or in the window.
- There is always waiter service in cafés, pubs and wine bars. In
  a pub you can also drink at the bar if you wish (cheaper).
- A service charge of 10–15% is almost always included on the
  bill (**BEDIENUNG INBEGRIFFEN**), but it is customary to
  leave some additional small change.
- Cafés serve non-alcoholic and alcoholic drinks, and are
  normally open all day.

WHAT TO SAY

I'll have . . . please	**Ich hätte gern . . . bitte** ish hetteh gairn . . . bitteh
a black coffee	**einen schwarzen Kaffee** inen shvar-tsen kaffeh
a coffee with cream	**einen Kaffee mit Sahne** inen kaffeh mit zahneh
a tea	**einen Tee** inen tay
with milk	**mit Milch** mit milsh
with lemon	**mit Zitrone** mit tsee-trone-eh
a glass of milk	**ein Glas Milch** ine glass milsh
two glasses of milk	**zwei Glas Milch** tsvy glass milsh
a hot chocolate	**eine heisse Schokolade** ineh hysseh shoko-lahdeh

a mineral water	ein Mineralwasser
	ine minerahl-vasser
a lemonade	eine Limonade
	ineh lim-o-nahdeh
a Coca Cola	eine (Coca) Cola
	ineh (coca) cola
an orangeade	einen Orangensprudel
	inen o-rung-shen-shproodel
a fresh orange juice	einen frischen Orangensaft
	inen frishen o-rung-shen-zaft
a grape juice	einen Traubensaft
	inen tra-ooben-zaft
an apple juice	einen Apfelsaft
	inen apfel-zaft
a beer	ein Bier
	ine beer
a draught beer	ein Bier vom Fass
	ine beer fom fass
a light ale	ein helles Bier
	ine hell-es beer
a lager	ein Pilsener
	ine pil-zen-er
a bitter	ein Altbier
	ine alt-beer
a brown ale	ein dunkles Bier
	ine doonk-les beer
a half	ein Kleines
	ine kly-nes
A glass of ...	Ein Glas ...
	ine glass
Two glasses of ...	Zwei Glas ...
	tsvy glass
red wine	Rotwein
	rote-vine
white wine	Weisswein
	vice-vine
rosé wine	Rosé
	rozay
dry	herben
	hair-ben
sweet	süssen
	soossen

A bottle of ...	**Eine Flasche ...**
	ineh flasheh
sparkling wine	**Schaumwein**
	sha-oom-vine
champagne (German)	**Sekt**
	zekt
champagne (French)	**Champagner**
	sham-panyer
A whisky	**Einen Whisky**
	inen visky
with ice	**mit Eis**
	mit ice
with water	**mit Wasser**
	mit vasser
with soda	**mit Soda**
	mit zoda
A gin	**Einen Gin**
	inen gin
with tonic	**mit Tonik**
	mit tonic
with bitter lemon	**mit Bitter Lemon**
	mit bitter lemon
A brandy/cognac	**Einen Weinbrand/Cognac**
	inen vine-brant/con-yac
A Martini	**Einen Martini**
	inen martini
A sherry	**Einen Sherry**
	inen sherry

These are local drinks you may like to try:

ein Schnapps	a strong spirit distilled from
ine shnaps	grain
eine Berliner Weisse	light Berlin ale with raspberry
ineh ber-leener vice-eh	juice
ein Himbeergeist	raspberry brandy
ine him-bear-gyst	
ein Doppelbock/Märzen	strong Munich beers
ine doppel-bock/mair-tsen	
eine Altbierbowle	a bitter with bits of pineapple
ineh alt-beer-boleh	
ein Kirschwasser	Black Forest brandy distilled
ine keersh-vasser	from cherries

ein Grog	hot diluted rum with sugar
ine gr*ok*	
ein Glühwein	mulled wine
ine gl*oo*-vine	
ein Malzbier	dark sweet malt beer
ine m*a*lts-beer	
ein Eierlikör	eggflip, eggnog
ine *eye*-er-leek*e*r	

Other essential expressions:

Miss! [*this does not sound abrupt in German*]	**Fräulein!**
	fr*oy*-line
Waiter!	**Herr Ober!**
	hair *o*-ber
The bill, please	**Die Rechnung, bitte**
	dee r*e*sh-noong b*i*tteh
How much does that come to?	**Wieviel macht das insgesamt?**
	v*ee*-feel makt das ins-gaz*a*mt
Is service included?	**Ist Bedienung inbegriffen?**
	ist bed*ee*noong *i*n-begriffen
Where is the toilet, please?	**Wo sind die Toiletten?**
	v*o* zint dee twa-l*e*tten

Ordering a snack

ESSENTIAL INFORMATION

- Look for any of these places:
  SCHNELLIMBISS ⎤
  IMBISSTUBE ⎦ (snack bar)
  BRATWURSTSTAND (sausage stall)
  HÄHNCHEN-GRILL (chicken takeaway; **WIENERWALD** is a popular chain)
  NORDSEE (a fish shop and takeaway chain found in larger towns)
- Apart from snacks, all these places sell soft drinks, canned or bottled beer, and also tea, coffee etc.
- Look for the names of snacks (listed below) on signs in the window or on the pavement.
- For cakes, see p. 62.
- For ice-cream, see p. 64.
- For picnic-type snacks, see p. 68.

WHAT TO SAY

I'll have . . . please	**Ich hätte gern . . . bitte** ish hetteh gairn . . . bitteh
a cheese sandwich/roll	**ein Käsebrot/Käsebrötchen** ine kaizeh-brote/kaizeh-brertshen
a ham sandwich/roll	**ein Schinkenbrot/ Schinkenbrötchen** ine shinken-brote/ shinken-brertshen
a roll with fish	**ein Fischbrötchen** ine fish-brertshen
an omelet	**ein Omelett** ine omelet
with mushrooms	**mit Pilzen** mit pil-tsen
with diced ham	**mit Schinken** mit shinken

These are some other snacks you may like to try:

eine Bratwurst	a fried spicy pork sausage
*i*neh br*a*ht-voorst	
eine Bockwurst	a large Frankfurter
*i*neh b*o*ck-voorst	
eine Currywurst	a grilled sausage topped with
*i*neh c*u*rry-voorst	curry and ketchup
ein halbes Hähnchen	half a (roast) chicken
ine h*a*lbes h*ai*n-shen	
ein Deutsches Beefsteak	a Hamburger steak
ine d*o*yt-shes b*ee*fsteak	
ein paar Spiegeleier	two fried eggs
ine par shp*ee*g-el-*eye*-er	
eine Gulaschsuppe	spicy beef soup
*i*neh g*oo*lash-z*oo*ppeh	

You may want to add to your order:

with bread, please	**mit Brot, bitte**
	mit br*o*te b*i*tteh
with chips	**mit Pommes Frites**
	mit pom fr*i*t
with potato salad	**mit Kartoffelsalat**
	mit kar-t*o*ffel-zal*a*ht
with (fried) onions	**mit Zwiebeln**
	mit tsv*ee*-beln
with mustard	**mit Senf**
	mit zenf
with ketchup	**mit Ketchup**
	mit k*e*tchup
with mayonnaise	**mit Mayonnaise**
	mit mayo-n*ai*zeh

[*For other essential expressions, see 'Ordering a drink', p. 80*]

In a restaurant

ESSENTIAL INFORMATION

- The place to ask for: **ein Restaurant** [see p. 19]
- You can eat at these places:
  RESTAURANT
  HOTEL-RESTAURANT
  GASTSTÄTTE/GASTHOF
  RASTHOF (motorway restaurant)
  GASTWIRTSCHAFT
  BAHNHOFSBÜFETT (at stations)
  GRILLSTUBE
  CAFÉ (limited choice here)
- By law, the menus must be displayed outside or in the window – and that is the *only* way to judge if a place is right for you.
- Self-service restaurants are not unknown, but most places have waiter service.
- A service charge of 10–15% is usually included in restaurant bills, but if satisfied with the service you should always leave some small change.
- Most restaurants offer small portions for children. Look for **KINDER-TELLER** (children's portions) on the menu.
- Hot meals are served from 12.00 to 2.00 p.m. at lunchtime and from 6.00 to 9.00–10.00 p.m. at night. After that many restaurants offer snacks for latecomers (soups, sausages, salads etc.) Ask for the 'small menu': **die kleine Karte** (dee kly-neh karteh).

WHAT TO SAY

May I book a table?	**Kann ich einen Tisch reservieren lassen?** kan ish *i*nen t*i*sh reser-*v*eeren lassen
I've booked a table	**Ich habe einen Tisch reservieren lassen** ish h*a*hbeh *i*nen t*i*sh reser-*v*eeren lassen

A table . . .	**Einen Tisch . . .** *i*nen t*i*sh . . .
for one	**für eine Person** foor *i*neh per-*zone*
for three	**für drei Personen** foor dr*y* per-*zonen*
The à la carte menu, please	**Die Speisekarte, bitte** dee shp*y*zeh-karteh b*i*tteh
The fixed-price menu	**Die Gedeck-Karte** dee gad*e*ck-karteh
The tourist menu	**Das Touristen-Menü** das tour*i*sten-men*oo*
Today's special menu	**Die Karte mit Tagesgedecken** dee k*a*rteh mit t*a*hg-es-gad*e*cken
What's this, please [*point to menu*]	**Was ist dies, bitte?** v*a*s ist d*ee*s b*i*tteh
The wine list	**Die Weinkarte** dee v*i*ne-karteh
A carafe of wine, please	**Eine Karaffe Wein, bitte** *i*neh ka-r*a*ffeh v*i*ne b*i*tteh
A quarter (250cc)	**Einen Viertelliter** *i*nen f*ee*r-tel-litre
A half (500cc)	**Einen halben Liter** *i*nen h*a*lben l*i*tre
A glass	**Ein Glas** ine glass
A bottle	**Eine Flasche** *i*neh fl*a*sheh
A half-bottle	**Eine halbe Flasche** *i*neh h*a*lbeh fl*a*sheh
A litre	**Einen Liter** *i*nen l*i*tre

Red/white/rosé/house wine	**Rotwein/Weisswein/Rosé/
	    Hauswein**
	r*o*te-vine/v*i*ce-vine/roz*ay*
	    h*o*use-vine

Some more bread, please	**Noch etwas Brot, bitte** nok *e*tvas br*o*te b*i*tteh
Some more wine	**Noch etwas Wein** nok *e*tvas v*i*ne
Some oil	**Etwas Öl** *e*tvas *e*rl

Some vinegar	**Etwas Essig** *e*tvas *e*ssick
Some salt	**Etwas Salz** *e*tvas *z*alts
Some pepper	**Etwas Pfeffer** *e*tvas pf*e*ffer
Some water	**Etwas Wasser** *e*tvas *v*asser
How much does that come to?	**Wieviel macht das insgesamt?** v*ee*-feel makt das ins-gaz*a*mt
Is service included?	**Ist Bedienung inbegriffen?** ist be-d*ee*n-ong *i*n-begriffen
Where is the toilet, please?	**Wo sind die Toiletten?** v*o* zint dee twa-*le*tten
Miss! [*This does not sound abrupt in German*]	**Fräulein!** fr*oy*-line
Waiter!	**Herr Ober!** hair *o*-ber
The bill, please	**Die Rechnung, bitte** dee r*e*sh-noong b*i*tteh

Key words for courses, as seen on some menus

[*Only ask this question if you want the waiter to remind you of the choice.*]

What have you got in the way of . . .	**Was für . . . haben Sie?** v*a*s foor . . . h*a*hben zee
STARTERS?	**VORSPEISEN** f*o*r-shpyzen
SOUP?	**SUPPEN** *zo*oppen
EGG DISHES?	**EIERSPEISEN** *ey*e-er-shpyzen
FISH?	**FISCHGERICHTE** f*i*sh-garisht-eh
MEAT?	**FLEISCHGERICHTE** fl*y*sh-garisht-eh
GAME?	**WILDGERICHTE** v*i*lt-garisht-eh
FOWL?	**GEFLÜGELGERICHTE** ga-fl*oo*gel-garisht-eh
VEGETABLES?	**GEMÜSE** ga-m*oo*zeh

CHEESE?	**KÄSE**
	k*a*y-zeh
FRUIT?	**OBST**
	opst
ICE-CREAM?	**EIS**
	ice
DESSERT?	**NACHSPEISEN**
	n*a*hk-shpyzen

UNDERSTANDING THE MENU

You will find the names of the principal ingredients of most dishes on these pages:

Starters, see p. 68   Fruit, see p. 71
Meat, see p. 75   Dessert, see p. 62
Fish, see p. 77   Cheese, see p. 68
Vegetables, see p. 71   Ice-cream, see p. 64

Used together with the following lists of cooking and menu terms, they should help you to decode the menu.
(These cooking and menu terms are for understanding only – not for speaking aloud.)

Cooking and menu terms

angemacht	in a special dressing
Auflauf	soufflé
blau	steamed and served with butter
blutig	rare
Bouillon	broth, clear soup
Brat–	fried
–braten	roast, joint
–brühe	broth
–brust	breast
Butter–	buttered
durchgebraten	well done
gebacken	baked
gedämpft	steamed
gedünstet (Austria)	steamed, stewed
gefüllt	stuffed
gegrillt	grilled
gekocht	boiled
in Gelee	jellied

gemischt	mixed
gepökelt	salted, pickled
geräuchert	smoked
gerieben	grated
geschmort	braised, stewed
gespickt	larded, smoked
halbdurch	medium
Hausfrauenart	with apple, sour cream and onions
hausgemacht	homemade
Holländisch	with mayonnaise
Holstein	topped with fried egg, garnished with anchovies and vegetables
Jägerart	served in red wine sauce with mushrooms
–Kaltschale	chilled fruit soup
–Kompott	stewed fruit
Kraftbrühe	broth, beef consommé
Kräuter–	with herbs
mariniert	marinated
Meerrettich–	with horse radish
Müllerin	baked in butter, dressed with breadcrumbs and egg
paniert	dressed with egg and breadcrumbs
Pell–	boiled in the jacket
Petersilien–	parsleyed
–püree	mashed
Rahm–	with cream
roh	raw
Röst–	fried
Sahne–	creamed
sauer	sour
Schlemmer–	for the gourmet
Schnitzel	escalope (of veal)
Senf–	with mustard
Sosse	sauce
Sülz–	in aspic
süss	sweet
überbacken	au gratin
Zwiebel–	with onions

Further words to help you understand the menu

Aalsuppe	eel soup, a speciality of Hamburg
Aufschnitt	sliced cold meat and sausages
Austern	oysters
Bauernomelett	bacon and onion omelette
Bierwurst	beer sausage
Birne Helene	vanilla ice-cream with pear and hot chocolate sauce
Bismarckhering	soused herring with onions
Blutwurst	black pudding
Bockwurst	large Frankfurter sausage
Bratkartoffeln	fried potatoes
Bratwurst	fried sausage (with herbs)
Deutsches Beefsteak	Hamburger steak
Eisbein	pig's knuckle
Ente	duck
Erbsensuppe	thick pea soup
Fasan	pheasant
Fleischkäse	type of meatloaf, sliced and fried
Forelle	trout
Frühlingssuppe	fresh vegetable soup
Gänseleberpastete	goose liver pâté
Gefrorenes	ice-cream specialities
Grünkohl	kale
Hackbraten	Hamburger steak
Kaiserschmarren	shredded pancake with raisins and almonds
Kartoffelpuffer	small potato and onion pancakes
Kasseler Rippenspeer	cured pork chops with mustard sauce
Klösse **Knödel**	dumplings
Königsberger Klopse	meat balls in a white caper sauce
Kohlrouladen	cabbage stuffed with minced meat
Labskaus	pork and potato stew served with fried eggs and gherkins
Lachs	salmon
Leberknödelsuppe	soup with liver dumplings
Leberwurst	liver pâté
Linsensuppe	lentil soup

Matjeshering	young salted herring
Ochsenschwanzsuppe	oxtail soup
Ölsardinen	tinned sardines
Paprikaschoten	green peppers
Pfannkuchen	pancake
Pfirsich Melba	peach with vanilla ice-cream, whipped cream, raspberry syrup
Räucheraal	smoked eel
Rauchwurst	smoked sausage
Rehrücken	saddle of deer
Rollmops	pickled herring fillet, rolled around onion slices
Rosenkohl	Brussels sprouts
Rösti	hashed brown potatoes
Röstkartoffeln	roast potatoes
Rote Beete	beetroot
Rotkraut	red cabbage
Rouladen	thin slices of meat, rolled up and braised in rich brown sauce
Russische Eier	hard-boiled eggs, with caper and mayonnaise dressing
Sardellen	anchovies
Sauerkraut	pickled white cabbage
Sauerbraten	beef marinated in vinegar, sugar and spices, and then braised
Schildkrötensuppe	turtle soup
Schinkenwurst	ham sausage
Schlachtplatte	assorted cold meat and sausages
Schweinshaxe	pig's knuckle
Serbische Bohnensuppe	spicy Serbian bean soup
Spargel	asparagus
Spätzle	South German variety of pasta
Speck	bacon
Strammer Max	raw ham and fried eggs, served on rye-bread
Truthahn	turkey
Weinbergschnecken	snails with garlic, herbs and butter
Wienerschnitzel	veal escalope in breadcrumbs

Health

ESSENTIAL INFORMATION

- For details of reciprocal health agreements between your country and the country you are visiting, visit your local Department of Health office at least one month before leaving, or ask your travel agent.
- In addition, it is preferable to purchase a medical insurance policy through the travel agent, a broker or a motoring organization.
- Take your own 'first line' first aid kit with you.
- For minor disorders, and treatment at a drug store, see p. 41.
- For finding your own way to a doctor, dentist, drug store, or Health and Social Security Office (for reimbursement), see p. 19.
- Once in Germany, Austria or Switzerland decide on a definite plan of action in case of serious illness: communicate your problem to a near neighbour, the receptionist or someone you see regularly. You are then dependent on that person helping you obtain treatment.
- In an emergency dial 110 for an ambulance service.
- If you need a doctor look for:
  ÄRZTE (in the telephone directory) or these signs:
  PRAXIS (surgery)
  ERSTE HILFE (first aid)
  KRANKENHAUS
  HOSPITAL } (hospital)
  UNFALLSTATION (emergency department of a hospital)

What's the matter?

I have a pain in my ...	**Ich habe Schmerzen ...**
	ish *h*ahbeh shm*ai*rts-en ...
abdomen	**im Unterleib**
	im *oo*nter-lipe
ankle	**im Fussgelenk**
	im *foo*ss-gal*e*nk
arm	**im Arm**
	im *a*rm
back	**im Rücken**
	im *roo*cken
bladder	**an der Blase**
	un der bl*a*h-zeh

I have a pain in my ...	Ich habe Schmerzen ...
	ish *h*ahbeh shm*ai*rts-en ...
bowels	im Darm
	im d*a*rm
breast	in der Brust
	in der br*oo*st
chest	im Brustkorb
	im br*oo*st-korp
ear	im Ohr
	im *o*r
eye	im Auge
	im *o*wg-eh
foot	am Fuss
	um f*oo*ss
head	im Kopf
	im k*o*pf
heel	an der Ferse
	un der f*ai*r-zeh
jaw	im Kiefer
	im k*ee*fer
kidneys	an den Nieren
	un den n*ee*ren
leg	im Bein
	im b*i*ne
lung	in der Lunge
	in der l*oo*ng-eh
neck	im Genick
	im gan*i*ck
penis	im Penis
	im p*ai*nis
shoulder	in der Schulter
	in der sh*oo*lter
stomach	im Magen
	im m*a*h-ghen
testicles	in den Hoden
	in den h*o*den
throat	im Hals
	im h*a*ls
vagina	in der Vagina
	in der v*a*hg-ee-nah
wrist	im Handgelenk
	im h*a*nt-galenk
I have a pain here [*point*]	Ich habe hier Schmerzen
	ish *h*ahbeh here shm*ai*rts-en

I have a toothache	**Ich habe Zahnschmerzen**
	ish hahbeh tsahn-shmairts-en
I have broken my dentures	**Mein Gebiss ist zerbrochen**
	mine gabis ist tsair-brocken
I have broken my glasses	**Meine Brille ist zerbrochen**
	mineh brilleh ist tsair-brocken
I have lost ...	**Ich habe ... verloren**
	ish hahbeh ... fer-loren
my contact lenses	**meine Kontaktlinsen**
	mineh kontakt-lin-zen
a filling	**eine Füllung**
	ineh foolloong
My child is ill	**Mein Kind ist krank**
	mine kint ist krank
He/she has a pain in his/her ...	**Er/sie hat Schmerzen ...**
	air/zee hat shmairts-en
ankle [see list above]	**im Fussgelenk**
	im fooss-galenk

How bad is it?

I'm ill	**Ich bin krank**
	ish bin krank
It's urgent	**Es ist dringend**
	es ist dring-ent
It's serious	**Es ist etwas Ernstes**
	es ist etvas airnstes
It's not serious	**Es ist nichts Ernstes**
	es ist nishts airnstes
It hurts	**Es tut weh**
	es toot vay
It hurts a lot	**Es tut sehr weh**
	es toot zair vay
It doesn't hurt much	**Es tut nicht sehr weh**
	es toot nisht zair vay
The pain occurs ...	**Der Schmerz tritt ... auf**
	der shmairts trit ... owf
every quarter of an hour	**alle Viertelstunde**
	alleh feertel-shtoondeh
every half-hour	**alle halbe Stunde**
	alleh halbeh shtoondeh
every hour	**jede Stunde**
	yaideh shtoondeh
every day	**jeden Tag**
	yaiden tahk

The pain occurs . . .	**Der Schmerz tritt . . . auf**
	der shmairts trit . . . owf
most of the time	**fast ununterbrochen**
	fast oon-oonter-brocken
I've had it for . . .	**Ich habe es seit . . .**
	ish hahbeh es zite . . .
one hour/one day	**einer Stunde/einem Tag**
	iner shtoondeh/inem tahk
two hours/two days	**zwei Stunden/zwei Tagen**
	tsvy shtoonden/tsvy tahg-en
It's a . . .	**Es ist ein . . .**
	es ist ine . . .
sharp pain	**stechender Schmerz**
	shteshen-der shmairts
dull ache	**dumpfer Schmerz**
	doompfer shmairts
nagging pain	**bohrender Schmerz**
	boren-der shmairts
I feel dizzy/sick	**Mir ist schwindlig/übel**
	meer ist shvindlik/oobel
I feel weak/feverish	**Ich fühle mich schwach/fieberig**
	ish fooleh mish shvak/feeb-rik

Already under treatment for something else?

I take . . . regularly [*show*]	**Ich nehme regelmässig . . .**
	ish nay-meh raig-el-masik . . .
this medicine	**dieses Medikament**
	deezes medikament
these tablets	**diese Tabletten**
	deezeh tabletten
I have . . .	**Ich habe . . .**
	ish hahbeh . . .
a heart condition	**ein Herzleiden**
	ine hairts-ly-den
haemorrhoids	**Hämorrhoiden**
	hemorro-ee-den
rheumatism	**Rheuma**
	roymah
I'm . . .	**Ich bin . . .**
	ish bin . . .
diabetic	**Diabetiker**
	dee-ah-beticker

asthmatic	Asthmatiker
	ast-mah-ticker
pregnant	schwanger
	shvanger
allergic to (penicillin)	allergisch gegen (Penicillin)
	allair-gish gay-ghen (peni-tsee-leen)

Other essential expressions

Please can you help?	Können Sie bitte helfen?
	kernnen zee bitteh helfen
A doctor, please	Einen Arzt, bitte
	inen artst bitteh
A dentist	Einen Zahnarzt
	inen tsahn-artst
I don't speak German	Ich spreche nicht deutsch
	ish shpresheh nisht doytsh
What time does . . . arrive?	Um wieviel Uhr kommt . . . ?
	oom veefeel oor kommt
the doctor	der Arzt
	der artst
the dentist	der Zahnarzt
	der tsahn-artst

From the doctor: key sentences to understand

Take this . . .	Nehmen Sie dies . . .
	nay-men zee dees . . .
every day/hour	täglich/stündlich
	taik-lish/shtoont-lish
twice/three times a day	zweimal/dreimal pro Tag
	tsvy-mal/dry-mal pro tahk
Stay in bed	Bleiben Sie im Bett
	bly-ben zee im bet
Don't travel . . .	Reisen Sie nicht . . .
	ryzen zee nisht . . .
for . . . days/weeks	in den nächsten . . . Tagen/ Wochen
	in den neksten . . . tahg-en/vok-en
You must go to hospital	Sie müssen ins Krankenhaus
	zee moossen ins kranken-house

Problems: complaints, loss, theft

ESSENTIAL INFORMATION

- Problems with:
  camping facilities, see p. 35   health, p. 93
  household appliances, see p. 39   the car, see p. 109
- If the worst comes to the worst, find the police station. To ask the way, see p. 19.
- Look for:
  POLIZEI (police)
  POLIZEIWACHE (police station)
- Ask for:
  FUNDBÜRO (lost property)
- If you lose your passport go to your nearest Consulate.
- In an emergency dial 110 (for police) or 112 (if there's a fire).

COMPLAINTS

I bought this ...	**Ich habe dies ... gekauft** ish hahbeh dees ... ga-kowft
today	**heute** hoy-teh
yesterday	**gestern** ghestern
on Monday [see p. 133]	**Montag** mone-tahk
It's no good	**Es ist nicht in Ordnung** es ist nisht in ort-noong
Look	**Sehen Sie** zay-en zee
Here [point]	**Hier** here
Can you ...	**Können Sie ...** kernnen zee
change it?	**es umtauschen?** es oom-towshen
mend it?	**es in Ordnung bringen?** es in ort-noong bring-en
Here's the receipt	**Hier ist der Kassenzettel** here ist der kassen-tsettel

Can I have a refund?	**Kann ich das Geld zurückbekommen?**
	kan ish das ghelt tsoo-*rook*-bekommen
Can I see the manager?	**Kann ich den Geschäftsführer sprechen?**
	kan ish den gashefts-*foorer* shpreshen

LOSS

[See also 'Theft' below: the lists are interchangeable]

I have lost . . .	**Ich habe . . . verloren**
	ish *hahbeh* . . . fer-*loren*
my bag	**meine Handtasche**
	mineh han-*tasheh*
my bracelet	**mein Armband**
	mine *arm*-bant
my camera	**meine Kamera**
	mineh kamerah
my car keys	**meine Autoschlüssel**
	mineh owto-shloossel
my car logbook	**meinen Kraftfahrzeugschein**
	minen kraft-far-tsoyk-shine
my driving licence	**meinen Führerschein**
	minen foorer-shine
my insurance certificate	**meine Versicherungskarte**
	mineh fer-zisheroongs-karteh
my jewellery	**meinen Schmuck**
	minen shmoock
my keys	**meine Schlüssel**
	mineh shloossel
everything!	**alle meine Sachen!**
	alleh mineh zakhen

THEFT

[See also 'Loss' above: the lists are interchangeable]

Someone has stolen . . .	**Man hat . . . gestohlen**
	man hat . . . ga-shtolen
my car	**mein Auto**
	mine owto
my car radio	**mein Autoradio**
	mine owto-rahdio

Someone has stolen ...	**Man hat ... gestohlen**
	man hat ... ga-sht*o*len
my money	**mein Geld**
	mine ghelt
my necklace	**meine Halskette**
	m*i*neh h*a*ls-ketteh
my passport	**meinen Pass**
	m*i*nen p*a*ss
my radio	**mein Radio**
	mine r*a*hdio
my tickets	**meine Fahrkarten**
	m*i*neh f*a*r-karten
my travellers' cheques	**meine Reiseschecks**
	m*i*neh ryzeh-shecks
my wallet	**meine Brieftasche**
	m*i*neh br*ee*f-tasheh
my watch	**meine Uhr**
	m*i*neh *oo*r
my luggage	**mein Gepäck**
	mine gap*e*ck

LIKELY REACTIONS: key words to understand

Wait	**Warten Sie, bitte**
	v*a*rten zee b*i*tteh
When?	**Wann?**
	vann
Where?	**Wo?**
	vo
Your name?	**Ihr Name?**
	eer n*a*hmeh
Address?	**Adresse/Anschrift?**
	ah-dr*e*sseh/*u*n-shrift
I can't help you	**Ich kann Ihnen nicht helfen**
	ish kan *ee*nen nisht h*e*lf-en
Nothing to do with me	**Ich bin dafür nicht zuständig**
	ish bin daf*oo*r nisht ts*oo*-shtendik

The post office

ESSENTIAL INFORMATION

- To find a post office, see p. 19.
- Key words to look for:
  POST
  POSTAMT
  BUNDESPOST
- Look for this sign.
- For stamps look for the words **BRIEFMARKEN** or
  POSTWERTZEICHEN on a post office counter.
- Some stationeries and kiosks which sell postcards also sell stamps.
- Letter boxes in Germany, Switzerland and Austria are yellow, but
  you may still find some blue ones in Austria. A red point on some
  letter boxes indicates that they are emptied frequently, late at night
  (**SPÄTLEERUNG**) and also on Sundays.
- Plain stamped postcards and stamps can also be obtained from
  yellow vending machines situated outside post offices or at the back
  of phone boxes. Ask for **BRIEFMARKEN AUTOMAT** or look for
  the word **WERTZEICHENGEBER**.
- For poste restante you should show your passport at the counter
  maked **POSTLAGERNDE SENDUNGEN** in the main post office:
  a small fee is usually payable.

WHAT TO SAY

To England, please	**Nach England, bitte** nahk eng-lant bitteh

[Hand letters, cards or parcels over the counter]

To Australia	**Nach Australien** nahk owstrah-lee-en
To the United States	**In die Vereinigten Staaten** in dee ferine-nik-ten shtahten

[For other countries, see p. 137]

How much is ...	**Wieviel kostet ...** *vee*-feel k*o*stet ...
this parcel (to Canada)?	**dieses Paket (nach Kanada)?** d*ee*zes pah-k*a*te (nahk k*a*nadah)
a letter (to Australia)?	**ein Brief (nach Australien)?** *i*ne br*ee*f (nahk owstr*a*h-lee-en
a postcard (to England)?	**eine Postkarte (nach England)?** *i*neh p*o*st-k*a*rteh (n*a*hk *e*ng-lant)
Airmail	**Luftpost** l*oo*ft-post
Surface mail	**Normaler Tarif** norm*a*h-ler tah-r*ee*f
One stamp, please	**Eine Briefmarke, bitte** *i*neh br*ee*f-markeh b*i*tteh
Two stamps	**Zwei Briefmarken** tsv*y* br*ee*f-marken

One (50) Pfennig stamp	**Eine Briefmarke zu (fünfzig)**
	   Pfennig
	*i*neh br*ee*f-markeh tsoo
	   (f*oo*nf-tsik) pf*e*nnik

I'd like to send a telegram	**Ich möchte ein Telegramm**
	   aufgeben
	*i*sh m*e*rshteh ine tele-gr*a*m
	   *o*wf-gaiben

Telephoning

ESSENTIAL INFORMATION

- Public phone boxes (ÖFFENTLICHER FERNSPRECHER) are painted yellow and take coins. Foreign calls can only be made from boxes marked with a green disc and the words INTERNATIONAL or AUSLAND. This is how to use a public telephone:
  - take off the receiver
  - insert the money
  - dial the number (unused coins will be refunded)

- For a call to the UK dial 0044; the code to the USA is 001.

- If you need a number abroad ring inquiries (AUSKUNFT) 00118. They normally speak English.

- For calls to countries which cannot be dialled direct go to a post office and write the country, town and number you want on a piece of paper. Add MIT VORANMELDUNG if you want a person-to-person call or R-GESPRÄCH if you want to reverse the charges.

- If you have difficulty in making a phone call, go to the post office and get them to put the call through (see above).

WHAT TO SAY

Where can I make a
  telephone call?
Local/abroad

Wo kann ich telefonieren?
vo kan ish tele-foneeren
**Ein Ortsgespräch/ein
  Auslandsgespräch**
ine orts-gashpraish/ine
  ows-lants-gashpraish

I'd like this number ... [*show number*]	Ich möchte diese Nummer ... ish mershteh deezeh noommer ...
in England	in England in eng-lant
in Canada	in Kanada in kanadah
in the USA	in den Vereinigten Staaten in den ferine-nik-ten shtahten

[*For other countries, see p. 137*]

Can you dial it for me, please?	Können Sie für mich wählen? kernnen zee foor mish vay-len
How much is it?	Wieviel kostet es? vee-feel kostet es
Hello!	Hallo! hullo
May I speak to ... ?	Kann ich ... sprechen? kan ish ... shpreshen
Extension ...	Apparat ... apparaht ...
I'm sorry, I don't speak German	Es tut mir leid, ich spreche nicht Deutsch es toot meer lite ish shpresheh nisht doytsh
Do you speak English?	Sprechen Sie Englisch? shpreshen zee eng-lish
Thank you, I'll phone back	Danke, ich rufe wieder an dankeh ish roofeh veeder un
Good-bye	Auf Wiederhören owf veeder-hern

LIKELY REACTIONS

That's (4) marks (50)	Das macht (vier) Mark (fünfzig) das makt (feer) mark (foonf-tsik)
Cabin number (3)	Kabine Nummer (drei) kabeeneh noommer (dry)

[*For numbers, see p. 129*]

Don't hang up	**Bleiben Sie am Apparat**
	blyben zee am appa-*ra*ht
I'm trying to connect you	**Ich verbinde Sie**
	ish fer-*bin*-deh zee
You're through	**Hier ist Ihre Verbindung**
	here ist *ee*reh fer-*bin*-doong
There's a delay	**Sie müssen warten**
	zee m*oo*ssen v*a*rten
I'll try again	**Ich versuche es noch einmal**
	ish fer-*zook*eh es nok *i*ne-mahl

Changing checks and money

ESSENTIAL INFORMATION

- Finding your way to a bank or change bureau, see p. 19.
- Look for these words on buildings:
  BANK (bank)
  SPARKASSE (bank, savings-bank)
  WECHSELSTUBE
  GELDWECHSEL } (change bureau)
- Banks are normally open from 8.00 a.m. to 12.30 p.m. and from 2.30 to 4.00 p.m. on weekdays. On Thursdays they stay open until 5.30 p.m. They are closed on Saturdays and Sundays.
- Change bureaux at frontier posts, airports and larger railway stations are usually open outside regular banking hours.
- Changing money or travellers' checks is usually a two-stage process. The formalities are completed at a desk called **DEVISEN**; you will then be sent to the cashier (**KASSE**) to get your money.
- To cash your own normal checks, exactly as at home, use your credit card where you see the Eurocheque sign. Write in English.
- Have your passport handy.

WHAT TO SAY

I'd like to cash ...	**Ich möchte ... einlösen**
	ish mershteh ... ine-lerzen
this travellers' cheque	**diesen Reisescheck**
	deezen ryzeh-sheck
these travellers' cheques	**diese Reiseschecks**
	deezeh ryzeh-shecks
this cheque	**diesen Scheck**
	deezen sheck
I'd like to change this into German marks	**Ich möchte dies in deutsche Mark wechseln**
	ish mershteh dees in doytsheh mark vexeln

Here's ...	**Hier ist ...**
	here ist ...
my banker's card	**meine Scheckkarte**
	m*i*neh sh*e*ck-karteh
my passport	**mein Pass**
	mine pass

For excursions into neighbouring countries

I'd like to change this ...	**Ich möchte dies ... wechseln**
[*show bank notes*]	ish m*e*rshteh dees ... v*e*xeln
into Austrian schillings	**in österreichische Schillinge**
	in *e*rster-ry-kisheh sh*i*lling-eh
into Belgian francs	**in belgische Franken**
	in b*e*l-ghish-eh fr*a*nken
into Danish kroner	**in dänische Kronen**
	in d*a*-nisheh kr*o*-nen
into Dutch guilders	**in holländische Gulden**
	in holl*e*ndisheh g*oo*l-den
into French francs	**in französische Franken**
	in fran-ts*er*-zisheh fr*a*nken
into Swiss francs	**in Schweizer Franken**
	in shv*y*tser fr*a*nken
What's the rate of exchange?	**Wie ist der Wechselkurs?**
	v*ee* ist der v*e*xel-koors

LIKELY REACTIONS

Your passport, please	**Ihren Pass, bitte**
	*ee*ren p*a*ss b*i*tteh
Sign here	**Unterschreiben Sie hier**
	*oo*nter-shr*y*ben zee h*e*re
Your banker's card, please	**Ihre Scheckkarte, bitte**
	*ee*reh sh*e*ck-karteh b*i*tteh
Go to the cash desk	**Gehen Sie zur Kasse**
	g*a*y-en zee tsoor k*a*sseh

Car travel

ESSENTIAL INFORMATION

- Finding a filling station or garage, see p. 19.
- Is it a self-service station? Look out for:
  SELBSTBEDIENUNG or **SB**.
- Grades of gasoline:
  BENZIN
  NORMAL } (standard)
  SUPER (premium)
  DIESEL
  MOTORRADÖL
  MEHRBEREICHSÖL } (two-stroke)
- 1 gallon is about 4½ litres (accurate enough up to 6 gallons).
- The minimum sale is often 5 litres (often less at self-service pumps).
- Filling stations are usually able to deal with minor mechanical problems. For major repairs you have to find a garage **(REPARATURWERKSTATT)**.
- Unfamiliar road signs and warnings, see p. 123.

WHAT TO SAY
[*For numbers, see p. 129*]

(9) litres of ...	(Neun) Liter ...
	(noyn) litre ...
(20) marks of ...	Für (zwanzig) Mark ...
	foor (tsvan-tsik) mark ...
standard	Normal
	nor-mahl
premium	Super
	zooper
diesel	Diesel
	deezel
Fill it up, please	Volltanken, bitte
	folltanken bitteh
Will you check ...	Bitte prüfen Sie ...
	bitteh proofen zee ...
the oil	das Öl
	das erl

the battery	**die Batterie**
	dee batteree
the radiator	**das Kühlwasser**
	das kool-vasser
the tyres	**die Reifen**
	dee ryfen
I've run out of petrol	**Ich habe kein Benzin mehr**
	ish hahbeh kine ben-tseen mair
Can I borrow a can, please?	**Können Sie mir einen Kanister leihen?**
	kernnen zee meer inen kanister ly-en
My car has broken down	**Ich habe eine Panne**
	ish hahbeh ineh panneh
My car won't start	**Mein Wagen springt nicht an**
	mine vahg-en shprinkt nisht un
I've had an accident	**Ich habe einen Unfall gehabt**
	ish hahbeh inen oon-fal gahapt
I've lost my car keys	**Ich habe meine Autoschlüssel verloren**
	ish hahbeh mineh owto-shloossel fer-loren
My car is ...	**Mein Wagen steht ...**
	mine vahg-en shtait ...
one kilometre away	**einen Kilometer von hier**
	inen kilo-mater fon here
three kilometres away	**drei Kilometer von hier**
	dry kilo-mater fon here
Can you help me, please?	**Können Sie mir bitte helfen?**
	kernnen zee meer bitteh helf-en
Do you do repairs?	**Machen Sie Reparaturen?**
	mak-en zee repara-tooren
I have a puncture	**Ich habe eine Reifenpanne**
	ish hahbeh ineh ryfen-panneh
I have a broken windscreen	**Die Windschutzscheibe ist zerbrochen**
	dee vint-shoots-shybeh ist tsair-brocken
I don't know what's wrong	**Ich weiss nicht, woran es liegt**
	ish vice nisht voran es leekt
I think the problem is here ... [point]	**Ich glaube, es liegt hieran ...**
	ish gla-oobeh es leekt here-un ...

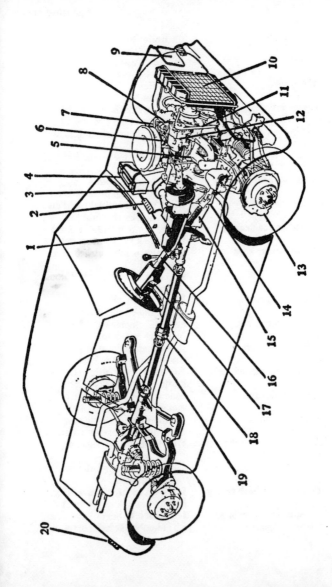

1 windscreen wipers	Scheibenwischer shyben-visher
2 fuses	Sicherungen zisher-oon-gen
3 heater	Heizung hy-tsoong
4 battery	Batterie batteree
5 engine	Motor mo-tore
6 fuel pump	Benzinpumpe ben-tseen-poompeh
7 starter motor	Anlasser un-lasser
8 carburettor	Vergaser fer-gahzer
9 lights	Scheinwerfer shine-vairfer
10 radiator	Kühler kooler

11 fan belt	Keilriemen kile-reemen
12 generator	Lichtmaschine lisht-masheeneh
13 brakes	Bremsen brem-zen
14 clutch	Kupplung koop-loong
15 gear box	Getriebe(block) ga-treebe(block)
16 steering	Lenkung lenk-oong
17 ignition	Zündung tsoon-doong
18 transmission	(Schalt-Getriebe (shalt)gatreebeh
19 exhaust	Auspuff ows-poof
20 indicators	Blinker blinker

Can you ...	**Können Sie ...**
	kernnen zee ...
repair the fault?	es reparieren?
	es repareeren
come and look?	es sich ansehen?
	es zish un-zay-en
estimate the cost?	einen Kostenvoranschlag machen?
	inen kosten-for-unshlahk mak-en
write it down?	es aufschreiben?
	es owf-shryben
How long will the repair take?	Wie lange wird die Reparatur dauern?
	vee langeh veert dee repara-toor dowern
When will the car be ready?	Wann wird der Wagen fertig sein?
	vann veert der vahg-en fair-tik zine
Can I see the bill?	Kann ich die Rechnung sehen?
	kan ish dee resh-noong zay-en
This is my insurance document	Hier ist meine Versicherungskarte
	here ist mineh fer-zisheroongs-karteh

HIRING A CAR

Can I hire a car?	**Kann ich einen Wagen mieten?**
	kan ish inen vahg-en meeten
I need a car ...	Ich brauche einen Wagen ...
	ish browkeh inen vahg-en ...
for two people	für zwei Personen
	foor tsvy per-zonen
for five people	für fünf Personen
	foor foonf per-zonen
for one day	für einen Tag
	foor inen tahk
for five days	für fünf Tage
	foor foonf tahg-eh
for a week	für eine Woche
	foor ineh vok-eh

Can you write down ...	**Können Sie mir ...** **aufschreiben?**
	kernnen zee meer ... owf-shryben
the deposit to pay?	**die Kautionssumme**
	dee kow-tsee-ons-zoommeh
the charge per kilometre?	**die Gebühr pro Kilometer**
	dee gaboor pro kilo-mater
the daily charge?	**die Gebühr pro Tag**
	dee gaboor pro tahk
the cost of insurance?	**die Versicherungskosten**
	dee fer-zisheroongs-kosten
Can I leave it in (Hamburg)?	**Kann ich ihn in (Hamburg)** **abliefern?**
	kan ish een in (hum-boorg) *up-leefern*
What documents do I need?	**Was für Unterlagen brauche ich?**
	vas foor oonter-lahg-en browkeh *ish*

LIKELY REACTIONS

I don't do repairs	**Wir machen keine Reparaturen**
	veer mak-en kineh repara-tooren
Where's your car?	**Wo steht Ihr Wagen?**
	vo shtait eer vahg-en
What make is it?	**Was für ein Wagen ist es?**
	vas foor ine vahg-en ist es
Come back tomorrow/on Monday	**Kommen Sie morgen/Montag** **wieder**
	kommen zee morgen/mone-tahk *veeder*

[For days of the week, see p. 133]

We don't hire cars	**Wir vermieten keine Wagen**
	veer fer-meeten kineh vahg-en
Your driving licence, please	**Ihren Führerschein, bitte**
	eeren foorer-shine bitteh
The mileage is unlimited	**Die Kilometerzahl ist unbegrenzt**
	dee kilo-mater-tsahl ist *oon-begrentst*

Public transport

ESSENTIAL INFORMATION

- Finding the way to the bus station, a bus stop, a trolley stop, the railway station and a taxi stand, see p. 19.
- Remember that lining up for buses is unheard of!
- To get a taxi you usually have to telephone the local **TAXIZENTRALE** (taxi centre) or go to a taxi stand. Hailing a taxi is less common and doesn't always work.
- Types of trains:
  Tee (Trans-Europe-Express; luxury high-speed train with first class only)
  INTERCITY
  EXPRESS
  SCHNELLZUG } (long distance trains, often between countries, stopping only at principal stations)
  D-ZUG
  EILZUG (medium-distance, internal train, stopping only at bigger towns)
  PERSONENZUG (slow local train, stopping at all stations)
  NAHVERKEHRSZUG (short distance train, often to suburbs)
- Key words on signs: [see also p. 123]
  FAHRKARTEN (tickets, ticket office)
  EINGANG (entrance)
  AUSGANG (exit)
  VERBOTEN (forbidden)
  GLEIS (platform, literally: track)
  BAHNSTEIG (platform)
  BAHNHOFSMISSION (Travellers' Aid Office)
  AUSKUNFT (information, information office)
  DB (initials for German railways)
  GEPÄCKAUFBEWAHRUNG (left-luggage)
  BUSHALTESTELLE (bus-stop)
  ABFAHRT (timetable, departures)
  ANKUNFT (timetable, arrivals)
  GEPÄCKABFERTIGUNG } (luggage office/forwarding office)
  GEPÄCKANNAHME
- Buying a ticket:
  Buy your train ticket at the ticket office inside the station. When travelling by bus or tram you usually pay as you enter.

When travelling by underground (**U-BAHN**) you buy your ticket from an automatic machine at the station. This also applies to trolleys in the larger cities where there is a ticket machine at each trolley stop.

In most German cities you can purchase a ticket which allows you to interchange between trolleys, underground and buses, in the one direction. (These can often be bought at smoke shops.) You can also buy a 'Rover'-ticket for a specified number of days; ask for a **TOURISTEN-FAHRKARTE** (toor*i*sten-far-karteh) at a main station ticket office.

WHAT TO SAY

Where does the train for (Bonn) leave from?	**Auf welchem Gleis fährt der Zug nach (Bonn) ab?** owf velshem gl*y*ss fairt der ts*oo*k nahk (bonn) up
At what time does the train leave for (Bonn)?	**Wann fährt der Zug nach (Bonn) ab?** vann fairt der ts*oo*k nahk (bonn) up
At what time does the train arrive in (Bonn)?	**Wann kommt der Zug in (Bonn) an?** vann kommt der ts*oo*k in (bonn) un
Is this the train for (Bonn)?	**Ist dies der Zug nach (Bonn)?** ist d*ee*s der ts*oo*k nahk (bonn)
Where does the bus for (Köln) leave from?	**Wo fährt der Bus nach (Köln) ab?** vo fairt der b*oo*s nahk (kerln) up
At what time does the bus leave for (Köln)?	**Wann fährt der Bus nach (Köln) ab?** vann fairt der b*oo*s nahk (kerln) up
At what time does the bus arrive at (Köln)?	**Wann kommt der Bus in (Köln) an?** vann kommt der b*oo*s in (kerln) un
Is this the bus for (Köln)?	**Ist dies der Bus nach (Köln)?** ist d*ee*s der b*oo*s nahk (kerln)
Do I have to change?	**Muss ich umsteigen?** moos ish *oo*m-shtyg-en

Where does . . . leave from?	**Wo fährt . . . ab?**
	vo fairt . . . up
the bus	**der Bus**
	der boos
the train	**der Zug**
	der tsook
the underground	**die U–Bahn**
	dee oo-bahn
for the airport	**zum Flughafen**
	tsoom flook-hahfen
for the cathedral	**zur Kathedrale/zum Dom**
	tsoor ka-teh-drahleh/tsoom dome
for the beach	**zum Strand**
	tsoom shtrant
for the market place	**zum Marktplatz**
	tsoom markt-plats
for the railway station	**zum Bahnhof**
	tsoom bahn-hof
for the town centre	**zur Stadtmitte**
	tsoor shtatt-mitteh
for the town hall	**zum Rathaus**
	tsoom raht-house
for St John's church	**zur Johanneskirche**
	tsoor yo-hannes-keersheh
for the swimming pool	**zum Schwimmbad**
	tsoom shvimm-baht
Is this . . .	**Ist dies . . .**
	ist dees . . .
the bus for the market place?	**der Bus zum Marktplatz?**
	der boos tsoom markt-plats
the tram for the railway station?	**die Strassenbahn zum Bahnhof?**
	dee shtrahssen-bahn tsoom bahn-hof
Where can I get a taxi?	**Wo kann ich ein Taxi bekommen?**
	vo kan ish ine taxi bekommen
Can you put me off at the right stop, please?	**Können Sie mir bitte sagen, wann ich aussteigen muss?**
	kernnen zee meer bitteh zahg-en vann ish ows-shtyg-en moos
Can I book a seat?	**Kann ich einen Sitzplatz reservieren?**
	kann ish inen zits-plats reserveeren

A single	**Eine einfache Fahrt**
	*ine*h *ine*-fak-eh fart
A return	**Eine Rückfahrkarte**
	*ine*h *r*ook-far-karteh
First class	**Erster Klasse**
	*air*ster kl*a*sseh
Second class	**Zweiter Klasse**
	tsv*y*-ter kl*a*sseh
One adult	**Ein Erwachsener**
	ine er-v*a*ksen-er
Two adults	**Zwei Erwachsene**
	tsv*y* er-v*a*ksen-eh
and one child	**und ein Kind**
	oont ine k*i*nt
and two children	**und zwei Kinder**
	oont tsv*y* k*i*n-der
How much is it?	**Wieviel kostet das?**
	vee-feel k*o*stet das

LIKELY REACTIONS

Over there	**Dort drüben**
	dort dr*oo*ben
Here	**Hier**
	here
Platform (1)	**Gleis/Bahnsteig (Eins)**
	glyss/b*a*hn-shtyk (*i*nes)
At (four) o'clock	**Um (vier) Uhr**
	omm (f*ee*r) *oo*r
[*For times, see p. 131*]	
Change at (Hanover)	**Steigen Sie in (Hannover) um**
	sht*yg*-en zee in (hann-*o*fer) oom
Change at (the town hall)	**Steigen Sie am (Rathaus) um**
	sht*yg*-en zee um (r*a*ht-house) oom
This is your stop	**Hier müssen Sie aussteigen**
	h*e*re m*oo*ssen zee *o*ws-shtyg-en
There's only first class	**Es gibt nur erste Klasse**
	es geept noor *air*steh kl*a*sseh
There's a supplement	**Sie müssen Zuschlag zahlen**
	zee m*oo*sen ts*oo*-shlahk ts*a*hlen

Leisure

ESSENTIAL INFORMATION

- Finding the way to a place of entertainment, see p. 19.
- For times of day, see p. 131.
- Important signs, see p. 123.
- In the more popular seaside resorts, you pay to go on the beach (**Kurtaxe**) and to rent a **Strandkorb** (shown in picture)
- Smoking is generally forbidden in theatres and movies. In some large cities, however, there are special movies for smokers (often called **SMOKY**) where you will normally have to pay more for the privilege of being free to smoke.
- It is customary to leave one's coat at the coatroom in theatres.

WHAT TO SAY

At what time does ... open?	**Um wieviel Uhr wird ... geöffnet?**
	oom veefeel oor veert ... ga-erffnet
the art gallery	**die Kunstgalerie**
	dee koonst-galeree
the botanical garden	**der botanische Garten**
	der botah-nisheh garten
the cinema	**das Kino**
	das kee-no
the concert hall	**der Konzertsaal**
	der kon-tsairt-zahl
the disco	**die Diskothek**
	dee disco-take
the museum	**das Museum**
	das moo-zay-oom
the night club	**der Nachtklub**
	der nakt-kloop

the sports stadium	**das Stadion**
	das sht*ah*-dee-on
the swimming pool	**das Schwimmbad**
	das shv*i*mm-baht
the theatre	**das Theater**
	das tay-*ah*ter
the zoo	**der Zoo**
	der tso
At what time does ... close?	**Um wieviel Uhr schliesst ...**
	oom v*ee*feel oor shl*ee*est ...
the art gallery	**die Kunstgalerie?**
	dee k*oo*nst-galer*ee*
[See above list]	
At what time does ... start?	**Um wieviel Uhr beginnt ...**
	oom v*ee*feel oor begh*i*nnt ...
the cabaret	**das Kabarett?**
	das kabar*e*tt
the concert	**das Konzert?**
	das kon-ts*ai*rt
the film	**der Film?**
	der f*i*lm
the match	**das Spiel?**
	das shp*ee*l
the play	**das Stück?**
	das sht*oo*k
the race	**das Rennen?**
	das r*e*nnen
How much is it ...	**Wieviel kostet es ...**
	v*ee*feel k*o*stet es ...
for an adult?	**für einen Erwachsenen?**
	foor *i*nen er-v*a*ksen-en
for a child?	**für ein Kind?**
	for ine k*i*nt
Two adults, please	**Zwei Erwachsene, bitte**
	tsvy er-v*a*ksen-eh b*i*tteh
Three children, please	**Drei Kinder, bitte**
	dry k*i*n-der b*i*tteh
[State price, if there's a choice]	
Stalls/circle	**Parkett/erster Rang**
	parkett/*ai*rster r*u*ng

Do you have ...	**Haben Sie ...** hahben zee ...
a programme?	**ein Programm?** ine pro-gramm
a guide book?	**einen Führer?** inen foorer
Where's the toilet, please?	**Wo sind die Toiletten?** vo zint dee twa-letten
Where's the cloakroom?	**Wo ist die Garderobe?** vo ist dee gardeh-robeh
I would like lessons in ...	**Ich möchte Unterricht nehmen im ...** ish mershteh oonter-risht naymen im ...
skiing	**Skifahren** shee-fahren
sailing	**Segeln** zaygeln
water skiing	**Wasserskifahren** vasser-shee-fahren
wind-surfing	**Windsurfen** vind-surfen
Can I hire ...	**Kann ich ... leihen** kan ish ... ly-en
some skis?	**Skier** shee-er
some skiboots?	**Skistiefel** shee-shteefel
a boat?	**ein Boot** ine bote
a fishing rod?	**eine Angel** ineh ung-el
a beach-chair?	**einen Strandkorb** inen shtrant-korb
the necessary equipment?	**die nötige Ausrüstung** dee nertig-eh ows-roostoong
How much is it ...	**Wieviel kostet es ...** veefeel kostet es ...
per day/per hour?	**pro Tag/pro Stunde?** pro tahk/pro shtoondeh
Do I need a licence?	**Brauche ich einen Erlaubnisschein?** browkeh ish inen erlowp-nis-shine

Asking if things are allowed

ESSENTIAL INFORMATION

- May one smoke here?
  May we smoke here?
  May I smoke here?
  Can one smoke here?
  Can I smoke here?
  Is it possible to smoke here?

  Kann man hier rauchen?

- All these English variations can be expressed in one way in German. To save space, only the first English version: **May one ... ?** is shown below.

WHAT TO SAY

Excuse me, please	**Entschuldigen Sie, bitte**
	ent-shool-dig-en zee bitteh
May one ...	**Kann man ...**
	kann man ...
camp here?	**hier zelten?**
	here tselt-en
come in?	**hereinkommen?**
	hair-ine-kommen
dance here?	**hier tanzen?**
	here tantsen
fish here?	**hier angeln?**
	here ung-eln
get a drink here?	**hier etwas zu trinken bekommen?**
	here etvas tsoo trinken bekommen
get out this way?	**hier hinausgehen?**
	here hinows-gay-en
get something to eat here?	**hier etwas zu essen bekommen?**
	here etvas tsoo essen bekommen
leave one's things here?	**seine Sachen hier lassen?**
	zineh zak-en here lassen
look around?	**sich umsehen?**
	zish oom-zay-en

May one ...	Kann man ...
	kann man ...
park here?	hier parken?
	here parken
picnic here?	hier picknicken?
	here pick-nicken
sit here?	sich hier hinsetzen?
	zish here hin-zetsen
smoke here?	hier rauchen?
	here rowken
swim here?	hier baden?
	here bahden
take photos here?	hier photographieren?
	here photograph-eeren
telephone here?	hier telefonieren?
	here telefon-eeren
wait here?	hier warten?
	here varten

LIKELY REACTIONS

Yes, certainly	Ja, gern(e)
	yah gairn(eh)
Help yourself	Ja, bitte
	yah bitteh
I think so	Ich glaube ja
	ish gla-oobeh yah
Of course	Natürlich
	nah-toor-lish
Yes, but be careful	Ja, aber seien Sie vorsichtig
	yah ahber zy-en zee for-zishtik
No, certainly not	Nein, auf keinen Fall
	nine owf kinen fahll
I don't think so	Ich glaube nicht
	ish gla-oobeh nisht
Not normally	Normalerweise nicht
	nor-mahler-vyzeh nisht
Sorry	Nein, tut mir leid
	nine toot meer lite

Reference

PUBLIC NOTICES

Key words on signs for drivers, pedestrians, travellers, shoppers and overnight guests.

ABFAHRT	Departures
ACHTUNG	Caution
ANKUNFT	Arrivals
ANLIEGER FREI	Access to residents only
ANMELDEFREIE WAREN	Nothing to declare
ANMELDEPFLICHTIGE WAREN	Goods to declare
ANMELDUNG	Reception
... AUF EIGENE GEFAHR	... at one's own risk
AUFZUG	Elevator
AUSFAHRT	Exit (from motorway)
AUSGANG	Exit
AUSKUNFT	Information office
AUSVERKAUF	Sale, clearance sale
AUSVERKAUFT	Sold out, full house
AUTOBAHN	Highway
BAD	Bathroom
BADEN VERBOTEN	No bathing
BAHNSTEIG	Platform
BAHNÜBERGANG	Level crossing
BAUSTELLE	Building site
BEDARFSHALTESTELLE	Bus-stop on request
BESETZT	Occupied (toilet); full (bus)
BETRETEN VERBOTEN	No trespassing
BETRIEBSFERIEN	Closed for holidays
BEWACHTER PARKPLATZ	Supervised car park
BITTE KLINGELN	Ring (bell)
BITTE KLOPFEN	Knock (door)
BITTE NICHT STÖREN	Do not disturb
BLAUE ZONE	Restricted parking zone
DAMEN	Ladies
DRÜCKEN	Push
DURCHFAHRT VERBOTEN	No through traffic
DURCHGANGSVERKEHR	Through traffic

DUSCHEN	Showers
EINBAHNSTRASSE	One-way street
EINFAHRT	Entrance, start of highway
EINGANG	Entrance
EINORDNEN	Get in lane
EINSTIEG VORN/ HINTEN	Enter at the front/at the rear
EINTRITT FREI	Admission free
EINWURF	Slot, put in . . .
ENDE (DER AUTOBAHN)	Motorway ends
ENGSTELLE	Road narrows
ENTWERTER	Ticket-stamping machine
ERDGESCHOSS	Ground floor
ERFRISCHUNGEN	Refreshments
ERSTE HILFE	First aid
ETAGE (ERSTE, ZWEITE, DRITTE)	Floor (first, second, third)
FAHRKARTENSCHALTER	Ticket office
FEIERTAGS GESCHLOSSEN	Closed on holidays
FERNSPRECHER	Public telephone
FEUERMELDER	Fire alarm
FREI	Vacant (toilet)
FREIBAD	Open air pool
FREMDENFÜHRER	Guide
FROSTSCHÄDEN	Road damaged by frost
FUNDBÜRO	Lost property
FUSSGÄNGERZONE	Pedestrian lane
GEBÜHREN	Fees, charges
GEFAHR	Danger
GEFÄHRLICHE KURVE	Dangerous curve
GEFÄHRLICHE STRÖMUNGEN	Dangerous currents
GEGENVERKEHR	Two-way traffic
GEÖFFNET	Open
GEPÄCKAUF- BEWAHRUNG	Left luggage
GEPÄCKTRÄGER	Porter
GESCHLOSSEN	Closed
GESCHWINDIG- KEITSGRENZE	Speed limit
GLEIS	Platform

HALT	Halt, stop
HEISS	Hot (tap)
HERREN	Gentlemen
HÖCHSTGE-SCHWINDIGKEIT	Maximum speed
HOCHGARAGE	Multi-storey car park
HUPEN VERBOTEN	No sounding of horns
KALT	Cold (tap)
KASSE	Cash desk
KEIN DURCHGANG FÜR FUSSGÄNGER	No pedestrians
KEIN TRINKWASSER	Not for drinking
KEIN ZUTRITT	No entry
KRANKENHAUS	Hospital
KREUZUNG	Crossroads
KUNDENDIENST	Customer service
KURVENREICHE STRECKE	Winding road
LANGSAM FAHREN	Drive slowly, slow down
LAWINENGEFAHR	Avalanche area
LEBENSGEFAHR	Danger of death
LEERUNG	Collection (mail)
LICHT EINSCHALTEN	Lights on
LIEGEWAGEN	Couchette
MÜNZEINWURF	Coin to put in
MÜNZRÜCKGABE	Returned coins
NICHT BERÜHREN	Do not touch
NICHTRAUCHER	Non-smoker (compartment)
NOTAUSGANG	Emergency exit
NOTBREMSE	Emergency brake
ÖFFENTLICHE TOILETTEN	Public conveniences
ÖFFNUNGSZEITEN	Opening hours
PARKEN NUR MIT PARKSCHEIBEN	Parking discs required
PARKEN VERBOTEN	No parking
PARKPLATZ	Car park
PARTERRE	Ground floor
POLIZEI	Police
PRIVATGRUNDSTÜCK	Private grounds
RADWEG	Bike path
RADWEG KREUZT	Bike crossing

RAUCHEN VERBOTEN	No smoking
RAUCHER	Smoking allowed
RECHTS FAHREN	Keep right
RESERVIERT	Reserved
ROLLTREPPE	Escalator
RUHETAG	Closed all day
RUTSCHGEFAHR BEI NÄSSE	Slippery surface in damp weather
SACKGASSE	Dead end
SCHLAFWAGEN	Sleepng car, sleeper
SCHLECHTE FAHRBAHN	Bad surface (road)
SCHLIESSFÄCHER	Luggage lockers
SCHLUSSVERKAUF	(Seasonal) sale
SCHNELLDIENST	Fast service
SCHULE	School
SEITENSTREIFEN NICHT BEFAHRBAR	Soft shoulders
SELBSTBEDIENUNG	Self-service
SONDERANGEBOT	Special offer
SPÄTVORSTELLUNG	Late showing
SPEISEWAGEN	Dining car
SPRECHSTUNDEN	Office hours
STEHPLÄTZE	Standing room
STEINSCHLAG	Falling stones
STRASSENARBEITEN	Road works
STRASSENGLÄTTE	Slippery surface (road)
TIEFGARAGE	Underground car park
TIEFPARTERRE	Basement, lower ground floor
TOILETTEN	Toilet
TRINKWASSER	Drinking water
U–BAHN	Underground (train)
ÜBERHOLEN VERBOTEN	Passing forbidden
UMLEITUNG	Detour
UNBEFUGTEN IST DAS BETRETEN VERBOTEN	Trespassers will be prosecuted
UNBESCHRANKTER BAHNÜBERGANG	Unguarded level crossing
VERBOTEN	Forbidden
VERKEHRSAMPELN	Traffic lights
VORFAHRT BEACHTEN	Yield
VORSICHT, BISSIGER HUND	Beware of the dog

VORSICHT VOR DEN ZÜGEN	Beware of the trains
WARTESAAL	Waiting room
WERKTAGS GEÖFFNET	Open on working days
ZIEHEN	Pull
ZIMMER FREI	Vacancies
ZIMMER ZU VERMIETEN	Room to rent
ZOLL	Customs
ZUTRITT VERBOTEN	No admission
ZU VERKAUFEN	For sale
ZU VERMIETEN	For hire, for rent

ABBREVIATIONS

ACS	**Automobil-Club der Schweiz**	Automobile Association of Switzerland
ADAC	**Allgemeiner Deutscher Automobil-Club**	General Automobile Association of Germany
Adr	**Adresse**	address
AG	**Aktiengesellschaft**	joint-stock company; corporation
AOK	**Allgemeine Ortskrankenkasse**	local health insurance office
AvD	**Automobil-Club von Deutschland**	Automobile Club of Germany
B	**Bundesstrasse**	A-road
Bayr	**Bayrisch**	Bavarian
Bhf	**Bahnhof**	railway station
BP	**Bundespost**	(Federal) Post Office
BRD	**Bundesrepublik Deutschland**	Federal Republic of Germany
C	**Celsius**	centigrade
DB	**Deutsche Bundesbahn**	German (Federal) Rail
DCC	**Deutscher Camping-Club**	German Camping Club
DDR	**Deutsche Demokratische Republik**	German Democratic Republic

DM	**Deutsche Mark**	German mark
DRK	**Deutsches Rotes Kreuz**	German Red Cross
DSG	**Deutsche Schlafwagen Gesellschaft**	German Sleeping Car Company
Frl	**Fräulein**	Miss
GmbH	**Gesellschaft mit beschränkter Haftpflicht**	limited company
Hbf	**Hauptbahnhof**	main railway station
JH	**Jugendherberge**	youth hostel
km	**Kilometer**	kilometre
LKW	**Lastkraftwagen**	lorry/truck
m	**Meter**	metre
Min	**Minute**	minute
MWSt	**Mehrwertsteuer**	value added tax
nachm	**nachmittags**	in the afternoon
ÖAMTC	**Österreichischer Automobil- Motorrad- und Touring-Club**	Austrian Automobile, Motorcycle and Touring Club
ÖBB	**Österreichische Bundesbahn**	Austrian (Federal) Rail
Pf(g)	**Pfennig**	pfennig
PKW	**Personenkraftwagen**	private motor car
Pl	**Platz**	(town) square
Rp	**Rappen**	Swiss centime
SB	**Selbstbedienung**	self-service
SBB	**Schweizerische Bundesbahn**	Swiss (Federal) Rail
St	**Stock**	floor, storey
Stck	**Stück**	piece, item
Std	**Stunde**	hour
Str	**Strasse**	street
tägl	**täglich**	daily
TCS	**Touring-Club der Schweiz**	Swiss Touring Club
U–Bahn	**Untergrundbahn**	underground railway
vorm	**vormittags**	in the morning
WC	**Wasser-Klosett**	toilet, lavatory

NUMBERS

Cardinal numbers

0	null	nool
1	eins	ines
2	zwei	tsvy
3	drei	dry
4	vier	feer
5	fünf	foonf
6	sechs	zex
7	sieben	zeeben
8	acht	ahkt
9	neun	noyn
10	zehn	tsain
11	elf	elf
12	zwölf	tsverlf
13	dreizehn	dry-tsain
14	vierzehn	feer-tsain
15	fünfzehn	foonf-tsain
16	sechzehn	zek-tsain
17	siebzehn	zeep-tsain
18	achtzehn	ahk-tsain
19	neunzehn	noyn-tsain
20	zwanzig	tsvan-tsik
21	einundzwanzig	ine-oont-tsvan-tsik
22	zweiundzwanzig	tsvy-oont-tsvan-tsik
23	dreiundzwanzig	dry-oont-tsvantsik
24	vierundzwanzig	feer-oont-tsvan-tsik
25	fünfundzwanzig	foonf-oont-tsvan-tsik
30	dreissig	dry-sik
35	fünfunddreissig	foonf-oont-dry-sik
36	sechsunddreissig	zex-oont-dry-sik
37	siebenunddreissig	zeeben-oont-dry-sik
38	achtunddreissig	akt-oont-dry-sik
39	neununddreissig	noyn-oont-dry-sik
40	vierzig	feer-tsik
41	einundvierzig	ine-oont-feer-tsik
50	fünfzig	foonf-tsik
51	einundfünfzig	ine-oont-foonf-tsik
60	sechzig	zek-tsik
61	einundsechzig	ine-oont-zek-tsik

70	siebzig	zeep-tsik
71	einundsiebzig	ine-oont-zeep-tsik
80	achtzig	ahk-tsik
81	einundachtzig	ine-oont-ahk-tsik
90	neunzig	noyn-tsik
91	einundneunzig	ine-oont-noyn-tsik
100	hundert	hoondert
101	hunderteins	hoondert-ines
102	hundertzwei	hoondert-tsvy
125	hundertfünfundzwanzig	hoondert-foonf-oont-tsvan-tsik
150	hundertfünfzig	hoondert-foonf-tsik
175	hundertfünfundsiebzig	hoondert-foonf-oont-zeep-tsik
200	zweihundert	tsvy-hoondert
250	zweihundertfünfzig	tsvy-hoondert-foonf-tsik
300	dreihundert	dry-hoondert
400	vierhundert	feer-hoondert
500	fünfhundert	foonf-hoondert
700	siebenhundert	zeeben-hoondert
1,000	tausend	towzent
1,100	tausendeinhundert	towzent-ine-hoondert
2,000	zweitausend	tsvy-towzent
5,000	fünftausend	foonf-towzent
10,000	zehntausend	tsain-towzent
100,000	hunderttausend	hoondert-towzent
1,000,000	eine Million	ineh mill-yon

Ordinal numbers

1st	erste	airsteh
2nd	zweite	tsvy-teh
3rd	dritte	dritteh
4th	vierte	feerteh
5th	fünfte	foonfteh
6th	sechste	zexteh
7th	siebte	zeepteh
8th	achte	ahk-teh
9th	neunte	noynteh
10th	zehnte	tsainteh
11th	elfte	elfteh
12th	zwölfte	tsverlf-teh

TIME

What time is it?	**Wie spät ist es?** vee shp*ai*t ist es
It's ...	**Es ist ...** es ist ...
one o'clock	**ein Uhr** *i*ne oor
two o'clock	**zwei Uhr** tsv*y* oor
three o'clock	**drei Uhr** dr*y* oor
four o'clock	**vier Uhr** f*ee*r oor
in the morning	**morgens** *m*orgens
in the afternoon	**nachmittags** n*a*hk-mittahks
in the evening	**abends** *a*h-bents
at night	**nachts** nakts
It's ...	**Es ist ...** es ist ...
noon	**zwölf Uhr mittags** tsverlf oor m*i*ttahks
midnight	**Mitternacht** mitter-nakt
It's ...	**Es ist ...** es ist ...
five past five	**fünf nach fünf** f*oo*nf nahk foonf
ten past five	**zehn nach fünf** ts*ai*n nahk foonf
a quarter past five	**viertel nach fünf** f*ee*rtel nahk foonf
twenty past five	**zwanzig nach fünf** tsv*a*n-tsik nahk foonf
twenty-five past five	**fünf vor halb sechs** f*oo*nf for halp z*e*x
half past five	**halb sechs** halp z*e*x

It's ...	Es ist es ist ...
twenty-five to six	fünf nach halb sechs foonf nahk halp zex
twenty to six	zwanzig vor sechs tsvan-tsik for zex
a quarter to six	viertel vor sechs feertel for zex
ten to six	zehn vor sechs tsain for zex
five to six	fünf vor sechs foonf for zex
At what time ... (does the train leave)?	Um wieviel Uhr ... (fährt der Zug ab)? oom veefeel oor (fairt der tsook up)
At ...	Um ... oom ...
13.00	dreizehn Uhr dry-tsain oor
14.05	vierzehn Uhr fünf feer-tsain oor foonf
15.10	fünfzehn Uhr zehn foonf-tsain oor tsain
16.15	sechzehn Uhr fünfzehn zek-tsain oor foonf-tsain
17.20	siebzehn Uhr zwanzig zeep-tsain oor tsvan-tsik
18.25	achtzehn Uhr fünfundzwanzig ak-tsain oor foonf-oon-tsvan-tsik
19.30	neunzehn Uhr dreissig noyn-tsain oor dry-sik
20.35	zwanzig Uhr fünfunddreissig tsvan-tsik oor foonf-oon-dry-sik
21.40	einundzwanzig Uhr vierzig ine-oon-tsvan-tsik oor feer-tsik
22.45	zweiundzwanzig Uhr fünfundvierzig tsvy-oon-tsvan-tsik oor foonf-oon-feer-tsik
23.50	dreiundzwanzig Uhr fünfzig dry-oon-tsvan-tsik oor foonf-tsik
0.55	null Uhr fünfundfünfzig nool oor foonf-oon-foonf-tsik

in ten minutes	**in zehn Minuten**
	in ts*ai*n min*oo*ten
in a quarter of an hour	**in einer Viertelstunde**
	in *i*ner f*ee*rtel-shtoondeh
in half an hour	**in einer halben Stunde**
	in *i*ner h*a*lben sht*oo*ndeh
in three quarters of an hour	**in einer Dreiviertelstunde**
	in *i*ner dry-feertel-shtoondeh

DAYS

Monday	**Montag**
	mone-tah*k*
Tuesday	**Dienstag**
	d*ee*ns-tah*k*
Wednesday	**Mittwoch**
	m*i*tt-vok
Thursday	**Donnerstag**
	d*o*nners-tah*k*
Friday	**Freitag**
	fry-tah*k*
Saturday	**Samstag/Sonnabend**
	z*a*ms-tah*k*/z*o*nn-ahbent
Sunday	**Sonntag**
	z*o*nn-tah*k*
last Monday	**letzten Montag**
	l*e*ts-ten mone-tah*k*
next Tuesday	**nächsten Dienstag**
	n*e*xten d*ee*ns-tah*k*
on Wednesday	**(am) Mittwoch**
	(um) m*i*t-vok
on Thursdays	**donnerstags**
	d*o*nners-tah*k*s
until Friday	**bis Freitag**
	bis fry-tah*k*
before Saturday	**vor Samstag/Sonnabend**
	for z*a*ms-tah*k*/z*o*nn-ahbent
after Sunday	**nach Sonntag**
	nah*k* z*o*nn-tah*k*
the day before yesterday	**vorgestern**
	f*o*r-ghestern

two days ago	**vor zwei Tagen**
	for tsv*y* t*a*hg-en
yesterday	**gestern**
	g*h*estern
yesterday morning	**gestern morgen**
	ghestern m*o*rgen
yesterday afternoon	**gestern nachmittag**
	ghestern n*a*hk-mittahk
last night	**gestern abend**
	ghestern *a*hbent
today	**heute**
	h*oy*-teh
this morning	**heute morgen**
	hoy-teh m*o*rgen
this afternoon	**heute nachmittag**
	hoy-teh n*a*hk-mittahk
tonight	**heute abend**
	hoy-teh *a*hbent
tomorrow	**morgen**
	m*o*rgen
tomorrow morning	**morgen früh**
	morgen fr*oo*
tomorrow afternoon	**morgen nachmittag**
	morgen n*a*hk-mittahk
tomorrow evening	**morgen abend**
	morgen *a*hbent
tomorrow night	**morgen abend**
	morgen *a*hbent
the day after tomorrow	**übermorgen**
	*oo*ber-morgen

MONTHS AND DATES

January	**Januar**
	y*a*h-noo-ahr
February	**Februar**
	f*ay*-broo-ahr
March	**März**
	mairts
April	**April**
	ah-pr*i*l

May	**Mai**
	my
June	**Juni**
	yoo-nee
July	**Juli**
	yoo-lee
August	**August**
	ow-goost
September	**September**
	zeptember
October	**Oktober**
	oktober
November	**November**
	november
December	**Dezember**
	detsember
in January	**im Januar**
	im yah-noo-ahr
until February	**bis Februar**
	bis fay-broo-ahr
before March	**vor März**
	for mairts
after April	**nach April**
	nahk ah-pril
during May	**im Mai**
	im my
not until June	**nicht vor Juni**
	nisht for yoo-nee
the beginning of July	**Anfang Juli**
	anfang yoo-lee
the middle of August	**Mitte August**
	mitteh ow-goost
the end of September	**Ende September**
	endeh zeptember
last month	**(im) letzten Monat**
	(im) letsten monaht
this month	**diesen Monat**
	deezen monaht
next month	**nächsten Monat**
	nexten monaht
in spring	**im Frühling/ Frühjahr**
	im frooling/froo-yar

in summer	**im Sommer** im *zo*mmer
in autumn	**im Herbst** im *hai*rpst
in winter	**im Winter** im *vi*nter
this year	**dieses Jahr** *dee*zes yar
last year	**letztes Jahr** *le*tstes yar
next year	**nächstes Jahr** *ne*xtes yar
in 1982	**neunzehnhundertzweiundachtzig** *no*yn-tsain-hoondert tsv*y*-oont-ahk-tsik
in 1985	**neunzehnhundertfünfundachtzig** *no*yn-tsain-hoondert *foo*nf-oont-ahk-tsik
in 1990	**neunzehnhundertneunzig** *no*yn-tsain-hoondert *no*yn-tsik
What's the date today?	**Welches Datum haben wir heute?** *ve*lshes *da*h-toom *ha*hben veer *ho*y-teh
It's the 6th of March	**Heute ist der sechste März** *ho*y-teh ist der *ze*xteh m*ai*rts
It's the 12th of April	**Heute ist der zwölfte April** *ho*y-teh ist der tsv*e*rlf-teh ah-pr*i*l
It's the 21st of August	**Heute ist der einundzwanzigste August** *ho*y-teh ist der *i*ne-oont-tsvansix-teh ow-g*oo*st

Public holidays

Unless otherwise specified, offices, shops and schools are closed on these days in Austria, Germany and Switzerland.

1 January	**Neujahrstag**	New Year's Day
6 January	**Dreikönigsfest**	Epiphany (Austria only)
•••	**Karfreitag**	Good Friday (Germany and Switzerland)
•••	**Ostermontag**	Easter Monday
1 May	**Tag der Arbeit**	Labour Day (Austria and Germany)
•••	**Himmelfahrt**	Ascension

...	**Pfingstmontag**	Whit Monday
...	**Fronleichnam**	Corpus Christi (Austria and some regions of Germany)
17 June	**Siebzehnter Juni**	Day of Unity (Germany)
15 August	**Mariä Himmelfahrt**	Assumption Day (Austria)
26 October	**Nationalfeiertag**	National Day (Austria)
1 November	**Allerheiligen**	All Saints Day (Austria)
...	**Buss-und Bettag**	Day of Prayer and Repentance (Germany)
8 December	**die unbefleckte Empfängnis**	Immaculate Conception (Austria)
24 December	**Heiligabend**	Christmas Eve (half day)
25 December	**erster Weihnachtstag**	Christmas Day
26 December	**zweiter Weihnachtstag**	Boxing Day
26 December	**Stephanstag**	St Stephen's Day (Austria and Switzerland)

COUNTRIES AND NATIONALITIES

Countries

Australia	**Australien** owstrah-lee-en
Austria	**Österreich** erster-rike
Belgium	**Belgien** belg-ee-en
Britain	**Grossbritannien** gross-britahn-ee-en
Canada	**Kanada** kanadah
Czechoslovakia	**die Tschechoslowakei** dee czechoslovak-y
East Africa	**Ostafrika** ost-afrikah
East Germany	**die DDR** dee deh-deh-air
Eire	**Irland** eer-lant

England	**England**
	eng-lant
France	**Frankreich**
	fr*a*nk-rysh
Greece	**Griechenland**
	gr*ee*shen-lant
India	**Indien**
	*i*nd-ee-en
Italy	**Italien**
	it*ah*l-ee-en
Luxembourg	**Luxemburg**
	l*oo*xem-boork
Netherlands	**Holland**
	h*o*llant
New Zealand	**Neuseeland**
	noy-z*ay*-lant
Northern Ireland	**Nordirland**
	nort-*ee*r-lant
Pakistan	**Pakistan**
	p*ah*-kistahn
Poland	**Polen**
	p*oh*l-en
Portugal	**Portugal**
	p*o*rt-oo-gahl
Scotland	**Schottland**
	sh*o*t-lant
South Africa	**Südafrika**
	zood-*a*frikah
Spain	**Spanien**
	shp*ah*-nee-en
Switzerland	**die Schweiz**
	dee shv*y*ts
to/for Switzerland	**in die Schweiz**
	in dee shv*y*ts
in Switzerland	**in der Schweiz**
	in der shv*y*ts
United States	**die Vereinigten Staaten**
	dee fer-*i*ne-nikten sht*ah*ten
to/for the United States	**in die Vereinigten Staaten**
	in dee fer-*i*ne-nikten sht*ah*ten
in the United States	**in den Vereinigten Staaten**
	in den fer-*i*ne-nikten sht*ah*ten
USSR	**die UdSSR**
	dee oo-deh-es-es-*ai*r

in/to/for the USSR	[as Switzerland]
Wales	**Wales**
	wales
West Germany	**Westdeutschland**
	vest-doytsh-lant
West Indies	**Westindien**
	vest-ind-ee-en
Yugoslavia	**Jugoslawien**
	yoogo-slahv-ee-en

Nationalities

[Use the first alternative for men, the second for women]

American	**Amerikaner/Amerikanerin**
	ameri-kah-ner/ameri-kah-ner-in
Australian	**Australier/Australierin**
	owstrah-lee-er/owstrah-lee-er-in
British	**Brite/Britin**
	breeteh/breetin
Canadian	**Kanadier/Kanadierin**
	kanah-dee-er/kanah-dee-er-in
East African	**Ostafrikaner/Ostafrikanerin**
	ost-afrikah-ner/ ost-afrikah-ner-in
English	**Engländer/Engländerin**
	eng-lender/eng-lender-in
Indian	**Inder/Inderin**
	inder/inder-in
Irish	**Ire/Irin**
	eereh/eerin
a New Zealander	**Neuseeländer/Neuseeländerin**
	noy-zay-lender/noy-zay-lender-in
a Pakistani	**Pakistaner/Pakistanerin**
	paki-stahn-er/paki-stahn-er-in
Scots	**Schotte/Schottin**
	shotteh/shottin
South African	**Südafrikaner/Südafrikanerin**
	zood-afrikah-ner/ zood-afrikah-ner-in
Welsh	**Waliser/Waliserin**
	vah-leezer/vah-leezer-in
West Indian	**Westinder/Westinderin**
	vest-inder/vest-inder-in

DEPARTMENT STORE GUIDE

Absatz-Bar	Heel bar
Alles für das Kind	Children's department
Auskunft	Information
Aussteuerartikel	Bridal room
Babyausstattung	Layette
Babynahrung	Baby food
Bastelabteilung	Do-it-yourself
Bettwäsche	Bedding, linen
Bilder und Rahmen	Paintings and frames
Blusen	Blouses
Brot	Bread
Bücher	Books
Büroartikel	Office supplies
Camping	Camping
Damenhüte	Millinery
Damenkonfektion/bekleidung	Ladies fashions
Damenwäsche	Lingerie
Delikatessen	Delicatessen
Dritte	Third
Elektrowaren	Electric appliances
Erdgeschoss	Ground floor
Erfrischungsraum	Refreshments
Erste	First
Etage	Floor
Fahrstühle	Lifts
Feinfrost	Frozen food
Fernsehen	Television
Frischfleisch	Fresh meat
Frisör	Hairdresser
Gardinen	Curtains
Geflügel	Poultry
Gemüse	Vegetables
Geschenkartikel	Gifts
Glas	Glassware
Haushaltswaren	Household goods
Heimwerker	DIY
Herrenartikel	Men(s)
Herrenkonfektion/bekleidung	Menswear
Kinderkonfektion/bekleidung	Children's clothes
Kosmetikartikel	Cosmetics
Kücheneinrichtung	Kitchen furniture
Kurzwaren	Haberdashery
Lampen	Lamps

Lebensmittel	Food
Lederwaren	Leather goods
Miederwaren	Girdles
Möbel	Furniture
Nähmaschinen	Sewing-machines
Oberhemden	Shirts (department)
Obst	Fresh fruit
Parfümerie	Perfumery
Pelze	Furs
Photoartikel	Photography
Porzellan	China
Putzmittel	Cleaning materials
Radio	Radio
Reisebüro	Travel agency
Rolltreppen	Escalators
Schallplatten	Records
Schmuck	Jewellery
Schnellimbiss	Snack bar
Schnittmuster	Paper patterns
Schreibwaren	Stationery
Schuhe	Shoes
Spielwaren	Toys
Spirituosen	Spirits, liquors
Sportartikel	Sports articles
Stock	Floor
Stoffe	Fabrics, drapery
Strickwaren	Knitwear
Strümpfe	Stockings
Süsswaren	Sweets
Tabakwaren	Tobacco
Teppiche	Carpets
Tiefgeschoss	Basement
Toilettenartikel	Toiletries
Trikotagen	Hosiery
Umtauschkasse	Exchange and refund
Untergeschoss	Basement
Vierte	Fourth
Weine	Wine
Werkzeuge	Tools
Wolle	Wool
Wurstwaren	Cold meats
Zeitungen	Newspapers
Zoo	Zoo
Zweite	Second

CONVERSION TABLES

Read the centre column of these tables from right to left to convert from metric to imperial and from left to right to convert from imperial to metric e.g. 5 litres = 8.80 pints; 5 pints = 2.84 litres.

pints		litres		gallons		litres
1.76	1	0.57		0.22	1	4.55
3.52	2	1.14		0.44	2	9.09
5.28	3	1.70		0.66	3	13.64
7.07	4	2.27		0.88	4	18.18
8.80	5	2.84		1.00	5	22.73
10.56	6	3.41		1.32	6	27.28
12.32	7	3.98		1.54	7	31.82
14.08	8	4.55		1.76	8	36.37
15.84	9	5.11		1.98	9	40.91

ounces		grams		pounds		kilos
0.04	1	28.35		2.20	1	0.45
0.07	2	56.70		4.41	2	0.91
0.11	3	85.05		6.61	3	1.36
0.14	4	113.40		8.82	4	1.81
0.18	5	141.75		11.02	5	2.27
0.21	6	170.10		13.23	6	2.72
0.25	7	198.45		15.43	7	3.18
0.28	8	226.80		17.64	8	3.63
0.32	9	255.15		19.84	9	4.08

inches		centimetres		yards		metres
0.39	1	2.54		1.09	1	0.91
0.79	2	5.08		2.19	2	1.83
1.18	3	7.62		3.28	3	2.74
1.58	4	10.16		4.37	4	3.66
1.95	5	12.70		5.47	5	4.57
2.36	6	15.24		6.56	6	5.49
2.76	7	17.78		7.66	7	6.40
3.15	8	20.32		8.65	8	7.32
3.54	9	22.86		9.84	9	8.23

miles		kilometres
0.62	1	1.61
1.24	2	3.22
1.86	3	4.83
2.49	4	6.44
3.11	5	8.05
3.73	6	9.66
4.35	7	11.27
4.97	8	12.87
5.59	9	14.48

A quick way to convert kilometres to miles: divide by 8 and multiply by 5. To convert miles to kilometres: divide by 5 and multiply by 8.

fahrenheit (°F)	centigrade (°C)		lbs/ sq in	k/ sq cm
212°	100°	boiling point	18	1.3
100°	38°		20	1.4
98.4°	36.9°	body temperature	22	1.5
86°	30°		25	1.7
77°	25°		29	2.0
68°	20°		32	2.3
59°	15°		35	2.5
50°	10°		36	2.5
41°	5°		39	2.7
32°	0°	freezing point	40	2.8
14°	−10°		43	3.0
−4°	−20°		45	3.2
			46	3.2
			50	3.5
			60	4.2

To convert °C to °F: divide by 5, multiply by 9 and add 32. To convert °F to °C: take away 32, divide by 9 and multiply by 5.

CLOTHING SIZES

Remember – always try on clothes before buying. Clothing sizes are usually unreliable.

women's dresses and suits

Europe	38	40	42	44	46	48
UK	32	34	36	38	40	42
USA	10	12	14	16	18	20

men's suits and coats

Europe	46	48	50	52	54	56
UK and USA	36	38	40	42	44	46

men's shirts

Europe	36	37	38	39	41	42	43
UK and USA	14	$14\frac{1}{2}$	15	$15\frac{1}{2}$	16	$16\frac{1}{2}$	17

socks

Europe	38–39	39–40	40–41	41–42	42–43
UK and USA	$9\frac{1}{2}$	10	$10\frac{1}{2}$	11	$11\frac{1}{2}$

shoes

Europe	34	$35\frac{1}{2}$	$36\frac{1}{2}$	38	39	41	42	43	44	45
UK	2	3	4	5	6	7	8	9	10	11
USA	$3\frac{1}{2}$	$4\frac{1}{2}$	$5\frac{1}{2}$	$6\frac{1}{2}$	$7\frac{1}{2}$	$8\frac{1}{2}$	$9\frac{1}{2}$	$10\frac{1}{2}$	$11\frac{1}{2}$	$12\frac{1}{2}$

Do it yourself

Some notes on the language

This section does not deal with 'grammar' as such. The purpose here is to explain some of the most obvious and elementary nuts and bolts of the language, based on the principal phrases included in the book. This information should enable you to produce numerous sentences of your own making. There is no pronunciation guide in most of this section partly because it would get in the way of the explanations and partly because you have to do it yourself at this stage if you are serious: work out the pronunciation from all the earlier examples in the book.

THE

All nouns in German belong to one of three genders: masculine, feminine or neuter, irrespective of whether they refer to living beings or inanimate objects.

The	masculine	feminine	neuter
the address		die Adresse	
the apple	der Apfel		
the bill		die Rechnung	
the cup of tea		die Tasse Tee	
the glass of beer			das Glas Bier
the key	der Schlüssel		
the luggage			das Gepäck
the menu		die Speisekarte	
the newspaper		die Zeitung	
the receipt		die Quittung	
the ham sandwich			das Schinkenbrot
the suitcase	der Koffer		
the telephone directory			das Telefonbuch
the timetable	der Fahrplan		

plural

die Adressen	the addresses
die Äpfel	the apples
die Rechnungen	the bills
die Tassen Tee	the cups of tea
die Gläser Bier	the glasses of beer
die Schlüssel	the keys
die Speisekarten	the menus
die Zeitungen	the newspapers
die Quittungen	the receipts
die Schinkenbrote	the ham sandwiches
die Koffer	the suitcases
die Telefonbücher	the telephone directories
die Fahrpläne	the timetables

Important things to remember

- There is no way of predicting if a noun is masculine, feminine or neuter. You just have to learn and remember its gender. Nouns ending in -ung, -keit and -heit are feminine and nouns ending in -chen or -lein are neuter, but this sort of rule is not very helpful because it accounts for relatively few words.
- In the tables, *the* is der before masculine nouns, die before feminine nouns, das before neuter nouns.
- Does it matter? Not unless you want to make a serious attempt to speak correctly and scratch beneath the surface of the language. You would be understood if you said das Speisekarte or die Fahrplan, providing your pronunciation was good.
- In the word list *the* is die before any noun in the plural (not to be confused with the feminine).
- There is no easy way of remembering how to spell German nouns in the plural. (To get into the right frame of mind, think of the plural of *ox, goose* and *sheep* in English.) Here are the six ways of making a noun plural:
    add -en, -n, or -nen
    change a vowel sound by putting on an umlaut ä, ö, ü
    don't add anything to the end
    add -er, usually with an umlaut on an a, o or u
    add -e, often with an umlaut on an a, o or u
    add -s to an imported foreign word like Hotel

● The methods are easy enough, but knowing which method to apply to which noun is a different matter. In this section, however, the spelling of nouns in the plural are given for you: try to learn them by heart as you meet and practise them.

Practise saying and writing these sentences in German:

Where is the key?	Wo ist der Schlüssel?
Where is the receipt?	Wo ist . . . ?
Where is the address?	
Where is the luggage?	
Where are the keys?	Wo sind die Schlüssel?
Where are the ham sandwiches?	Wo sind . . . ?
Where are the newspapers?	
Where are the apples?	

Now make up more sentences along the same lines. Try adding *please*: **bitte**, at the beginning or end.

! CAUTION
In phrases beginning
Have you got the . . . ?
I'd like the . . .
Where can I get the . . . ?
masculine singular nouns (e.g. apple, key, suitcase, timetable) pose a problem. Quite simply, the word for *the*: **der** has to change to **den**. (This is usually called the Accusative Case, but it affects only the masculine singular.) In the Accusative Case
der Apfel becomes **den Apfel**
der Schlüssel becomes **den Schlüssel**
der Koffer becomes **den Koffer**
der Fahrplan becomes **den Fahrplan**
(The plural is not affected)

Practise saying and writing these sentences in German. (Look out for the caution sign !)

! Have you got the key?	Haben Sie den Schlüssel?
! Have you got the suitcase?	Haben Sie . . . ?
Have you got the luggage?	
Have you got the telephone directory?	
Have you got the menu?	

! I'd like the key   **Ich möchte . . . Schlüssel**
! I'd like the timetable
  I'd like the bill
  I'd like the receipt
  I'd like the keys
! Where can I get the key?   **Wo kann man . . . Schlüssel**
                                       bekommen?

  Where can I get the address?
  Where can I get the timetables?

Now make up more sentences along the same lines.
Try adding *please*: **bitte,** at the beginning or end.

A/AN

A/an	masculine	feminine	neuter
an address		eine Adresse	
an apple	ein Apfel		
a bill		eine Rechnung	
a cup of tea		eine Tasse Tee	
a glass of beer			ein Glas Bier
a key	ein Schlüssel		
a menu		eine Speisekarte	
a newspaper		eine Zeitung	
a receipt		eine Quittung	
a ham sandwich			ein Schinkenbrot
a suitcase	ein Koffer		
a telephone directory			ein Telefonbuch
a timetable	ein Fahrplan		

plural	Some/any
Adressen	addresses
Äpfel	apples
Rechnungen	bills
Tassen Tee	cups of tea
Gläser Bier	glasses of beer
Schlüssel	keys
Speisekarten	menus
Zeitungen	newspapers
Quittungen	receipts
Schinkenbrote	ham sandwiches
Koffer	suitcases
Telefonbücher	telephone directories
Fahrpläne	timetables

Important things to remember

- In the tables, *a* or *an* is **ein** before a masculine noun, **eine** before a feminine noun, **ein** before a neuter noun.
- *Some* or *any* before a noun in the plural has no equivalent in German. Just leave it out.

! CAUTION

In phrases beginning
Have you got . . . ?
I'd like . . .
Where can I get . . . ?
Is there . . . ?
Are there . . . ?
I'll have . . .
I need . . .
masculine singular nouns pose a problem. The word for *a/an*: **ein** has to change to **einen**. In these examples (of the Accusative Case) only masculine singular nouns are affected
ein Apfel becomes **einen Apfel**
ein Schlüssel becomes **einen Schlüssel**
ein Koffer becomes **einen Koffer**
ein Fahrplan becomes **einen Fahrplan**
(The plural is not affected.)

Practise saying and writing these sentences in German. (Look out for the caution sign !)

Have you got a receipt?	**Haben Sie eine . . . ?**
! Have you got an apple?	
I'd like a telephone directory	**Ich möchte ein . . .**
! I'd like a timetable	
I'd like (some) ham sandwiches	
Where can I get a cup of tea?	**Wo kann mann eine . . . bekommen?**
! Where can I get a suitcase?	
Where can I get (some) newspapers?	
Is there a menu?	**Gibt es hier eine . . . ?**
! Is there a key?	**Gibt es hier . . . ?**
! Is there a timetable?	
Are there (any) keys?	**Gibt es hier . . . ?**
Are there (any) newspapers?	
Are there (any) ham sandwiches?	
I'll have a glass of beer?	**Ich hätte gern ein . . .**
I'll have a cup of tea	**Ich hätte gern . . .**
! I'll have an apple	
I'll have (some) apples	
I'll have (some) ham sandwiches	
I need a receipt	**Ich brauche eine . . .**
! I need a suitcase	
I need a cup of tea	
! I need a key	
I need (some) suitcases	
I need (some) addresses	
I need (some) ham sandwiches	

Now make up more sentences along the same lines.

SOME/ANY

In cases where *some* or *any* refer to more than one thing, such as *some/any newspapers* and *some/any tomatoes,* there is no German equivalent, as explained earlier:

Zeitungen	some/any newspapers
Tomaten	some/any tomatoes

As a guide, you can usually count the number of containers or whole items.

In cases where *some* refers to part of a whole thing or an indefinite quantity, the word etwas can be used. Neither the gender of the noun nor the Accusative Case pose problems. Look at the list below and complete it:

the butter	die Butter	etwas Butter	some butter
the bread	das Brot	etwas Brot	some bread
the cheese	der Käse	etwas Käse	some cheese
the coffee	der Kaffee	etwas Kaffee	some coffee
the ice-cream	das Eis	...	some ice-cream
the lemonade	die Limonade	...	some lemonade
the pineapple	die Ananas	...	some pineapple
the sugar	der Zucker	...	some sugar
the tea	der Tee	...	some tea
the water	das Wasser	...	some water
the wine	der Wein	...	some wine

(Etwas is not essential, however, and can just be left out altogether.)

Practise saying and writing these sentences in German:

Have you got some coffee?	Haben Sie etwas Kaffee?
	Haben Sie Kaffee?

Have you got some ice-cream?
Have you got some pineapple?
I'd like some butter.
I'd like some sugar.
I'd like some bread.
Where can I get some cheese?
Where can I get some
  ice-cream?
Where can I get some water?
Is there any lemonade?
Is there any water?
Is there any wine?
I'll have some butter.
I'll have some tea.
I'll have some coffee.
I need some sugar.
I need some butter.
I need some coffee.

THIS AND THAT

There are two words in German
dies   (this)
das   (that)
If you don't know the German name for an object, just point and say:

Ich möchte das	I'd like that
Ich hätte gern dies	I'll have this
Ich brauche das	I need that

HELPING OTHERS

You can help yourself with phrases such as:

I'd like . . . a ham sandwich	**Ich möchte . . . ein Schinkenbrot**
Where can I get . . . a cup of tea?	**Wo kann man . . . eine Tasse Tee . . . bekommen?**
I'll have . . . a glass of beer	**Ich hätte gern . . . ein Glas Bier**
I need . . . a receipt	**Ich brauche . . . eine Quittung**

If you come across a compatriot having trouble making himself or herself understood, you should be able to speak to a German person on their behalf.

He'd like . . .	**Er möchte ein Schinkenbrot**
	er *me*rshteh *i*ne sh*i*nken-brote
She'd like . . .	**Sie möchte ein Schinkenbrot**
	zee *me*rshteh *i*ne sh*i*nken-brote

Strictly speaking, **kann man . . . ?** means *can one . . . ?* and normally serves instead of *can I. . . ?* (kann ich. . . ?), *can he. . . ?, can she. . . ?, can they. . . ?* and *can we. . . ?* However, all the above-mentioned variations in German are included in the remainder of this section because of their potential usefulness.

Where can he get . . . ?	**Wo kann er eine Tasse Tee bekommen?**
	vo k*a*nn er *i*neh t*a*sseh tay bek*o*mmen
Where can she get . . . ?	**Wo kann sie eine Tasse Tee bekommen?**
	vo k*a*nn zee *i*neh t*a*sseh tay bek*o*mmen
He'll have . . .	**Er hätte gern ein Glas Bier**
	er h*e*tteh g*ai*rn *i*ne glass b*ee*r

She'll have...	**Sie hätte gern ein Glas Bier** zee hetteh gairn *i*ne glass b*ee*r
He needs...	**Er braucht eine Quittung** er bra-*oo*kt *i*neh kv*i*ttoong
She needs...	**Sie braucht eine Quittung** zee bra-*oo*kt *i*neh kv*i*ttoong

You can also help a couple or a group if *they* are having difficulties. The German word for *they* is also sie, but there is a difference, which is fairly easy to detect. (Elsewhere in this book you will have noticed that Sie can also mean *you*)

They'd like...	**Sie möchten (etwas) Käse** zee m*e*rshten (*e*tvas) k*a*y-zeh
Where can they get...?	**Wo können sie (etwas) Butter bekommen?** vo kernen zee (*e*tvas) b*oo*tter bek*o*mmen
They'll have...	**Sie hätten gern (etwas) Wein** zee hetten g*ai*rn (*e*tvas) v*i*ne
They need...	**Sie brauchen (etwas) Wasser** zee bra-*oo*ken (*e*tvas) v*a*sser

What about the two of you? No problem the word for *we* is **wir.**

We'd like...	**Wir möchten (etwas)Wein,** veer mershten (*e*tvas) v*i*ne
Where can we get...?	**Wo können wir (etwas) Wasser bekommen?** vo kernen veer (*e*tvas) v*a*sser bek*o*mmen
We'll have...	**Wir hätten gern (etwas) Butter** veer hetten g*ai*rn (*e*tvas) b*oo*tter
We need...	**Wir brauchen (etwas) Zucker** veer bra-*oo*ken (*e*tvas) ts*oo*cker

Try writing out your own checklist for these four useful phrase-starters, like this:

Ich möchte...	Wir möchten...
Er möchte...	Sie möchten...
Sie möchte...	
Wo kann ich...bekommen?	Wo...wir...?
Wo kann er...bekommen?	Wo...sie...?
Wo...sie...bekommen?	

MORE PRACTICE

Here are some more German names of things. See how many
different sentences you can make up, using the various points of
information given earlier in this section.

		singular	plural
1	ashtray	Aschenbecher (m)	Aschenbecher
2	ballpen	Kugelschreiber (m)	Kugelschreiber
3	bag	Tasche (f)	Taschen
4	bottle	Flasche (f)	Flaschen
5	car	Auto (n)	Autos
6	cigarette	Zigarette (f)	Zigaretten
7	corkscrew	Korkenzieher (m)	Korkenzieher
8	egg	Ei (n)	Eier
9	house	Haus (n)	Häuser
10	knife	Messer (n)	Messer
11	mountain	Berg (m)	Berge
12	plate	Teller (m)	Teller
13	postcard	Postkarte (f)	Postkarten
14	room	Zimmer (n)	Zimmer
15	shoe	Schuh (m)	Schuhe
16	stamp	Briefmarke (f)	Briefmarken
17	street	Strasse (f)	Strassen
18	ticket	Fahrkarte (f)	Fahrkarten
19	train	Zug (m)	Züge
20	wallet	Brieftasche (f)	Brieftaschen

Index

LANGUAGE AND TRAVEL BOOKS
FROM PASSPORT BOOKS

Multilingual
The Insult Dictionary:
   How to Give 'Em Hell in 5 Nasty Languages
The Lover's Dictionary:
   How to be Amorous in 5 Delectable Languages
Multilingual Phrase Book
International Traveler's Phrasebook

Spanish
Vox Spanish and English Dictionaries
Harrap's Concise Spanish and English Dictionary
The Spanish Businessmate
Nice 'n Easy Spanish Grammar
Spanish Verbs and Essentials of Grammar
Getting Started in Spanish
Spanish Verb Drills
Guide to Spanish Idioms
Guide to Correspondence in Spanish
Español para los Hispanos
Diccionario Básico Norteamericano

French
Harrap's French and English Dictionaries
French Verbs and Essentials of Grammar
Getting Started in French
French Verb Drills
Guide to Correspondence in French
The French Businessmate
Nice 'n Easy French Grammar

German
New Schöffler-Weis German and English Dictionary
Klett German and English Dictionary
Harrap's Concise German and English Dictionary
Getting Started in German
German Verb Drills
German Verbs and Essentials of Grammar
The German Businessmate
Nice 'n Easy German Grammar

Italian
Getting Started in Italian
Italian Verbs and Essentials of Grammar

Russian
Russian Essentials of Grammar
Business Russian

Japanese
Japanese in Plain English
Everyday Japanese

Just Listen 'n Learn Language Programs
Complete Courses in Spanish, French,
   German, Italian and Greek

Travel and Reference
Nagel's Encyclopedia Guides
World at Its Best Travel Series
Mystery Reader's Walking Guide: London
Business Capitals of the World
European Atlas
Health Guide for International Travelers
Passport's Japan Almanac
Passport's Travel Paks
Japan Today
British/American Language Dictionary
Bon Voyage!
Hiking and Walking Guide to Europe

PASSPORT BOOKS

Trade Imprint of National Textbook Company
4255 West Touhy Avenue
Lincolnwood, Illinois 60646-1975 U.S.A.